19th Century
PLAINS INDIAN DRESSES
by Susan Jennys

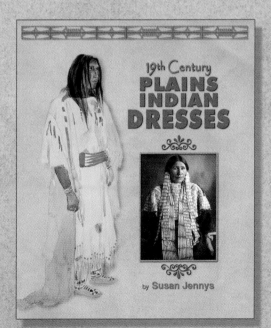

Slow Bull's wife, Sioux, wearing a "saved list" tradecloth dress decorated with dentalium shells, which are also used for the earrings. A simple belt, bone hairpipe breastplate and hairpipe and bead necklace worn "bandolier" style complete the outfit. Photo courtesy of Library of Congress, #LCUSZ62-50160.

About the Cover

"Piegan Blackfeet Woman" – Karl Bodmer watercolor, ca 1833. Clothed in a typically decorated, two-skin dress popular on the Northern Plains in the first half of the nineteenth century, this woman's moccasins, leggings, belt and bracelets are all clearly shown. Her husband allowed her to pose in return for a gift of vermilion and glass beads. Joslyn Art Museum, Omaha Nebraska #1986-49-292

Inset Photo- Mrs. Jack Treetop, Sioux, appears on page 59 with description. Fiske photo, ca. 1908, courtesy of State Historical Society of North Dakota.

Panoramic view of Sioux women dancing in all their finery— calico dresses and shawls, tanned hide dresses with elaborate beadwork, saved-list cloth dresses decorated with either genuine or carved bone elk teeth and dentalium shells. Rosebud Reservation, South Dakota. Photo courtesy of Marquette University Libraries, Bureau of Catholic Indian Missions Records. Photographer Unknown. Negative No. 1643

Published by Crazy Crow Trading Post

P.O. Box 847, Pottsboro, Texas 75076
(903) 786-2287   www.crazycrow.com

**Edited by Earl and Faith Fenner,
Benson Lanford, & Rex Reddick**

Bob Sanford, Art Director

**Artwork by Alexander Koslov,
Ed Wells & Jessica Reddick**

**Layout Design and Typography by
Bob Sanford & Rex Reddick**

ISBN 1-929572-01-8

19th Century Plains Indian Dresses

Table of Contents

Chipeta, Wife of Ute Chief Ouray

She is wearing her fancy dress for a visit to Washington, D.C., circa 1868, in a painting by Robert Lindneux. Although not shown in the painting, an actual photograph of this dress reveals the characteristic mountain sheep tail of the two-skin dress. *From a photograph in the author's collection.*

19th Century Plains Indian Dresses

INTRODUCTION

It has been said that clothing is a window to the human soul. In other words, what we wear is a reflection of many things: our age and social position, our idea of comfort, and our personal interpretation of what our culture refers to as "style." Fashion is far from static — trends and innovations come and go. The same is also true of historic fashion. The clothing of the Indians of the American Great Plains during the 1800s has been studied and admired by countless students and scholars over the years. Rather than taking a clinical academic approach, many of these studies have instead been focused on elegance and beauty and have offered us a glimpse into the very soul of these people. It is my hope that the book you are now holding will be one such glimpse.

Plains Indian women's garments from the 19th century are among the most elegant pieces of attire any woman could hope to own and wear. In this book you will be introduced to dresses from the Blackfoot, Crow, Sioux, Shoshoni, Ute, Nez Perce, Comanche, Cheyenne and Arapaho traditions, along with a brief history of the various styles. The primary focus will be on four basic styles of specific museum examples. These will be compared to and contrasted with other examples, so that you can approach them in context to each other. Most importantly, the tools you will be given in this book will enable you to reproduce several of the basic historic dress styles, as well as pairing them with appropriately related accessories.

The stunning beauty of 19th century Plains Indian women's garments is not only a feast for the eyes, but is also both a testimony to the artistic abilities of the artists and a window to their souls.

I would like to make it plain from the very beginning that I do not advocate the exact copying of any decoration or embellishment of historic material culture. Not only do ethical considerations come to play in this issue, but for me the bottom line is respect. The beautiful historic garments and accessories you will be introduced to here are reflections of the individuals who produced and wore them. The same could be said about your work. The important thing to remember when re-creating historic clothing is to be well-studied enough as a crafter to be able to produce an item in a style that is at once recognizable (i.e., 1870's Kiowa, 1860's Blackfoot, etc.) but that bears your historically viable interpretation of embellishment within that same parameter. Historical credibility can be maintained without sacrificing respect.

A word about terminology: the terms "Native American" and "American Indian" are used interchangeably in this book. In this ongoing word-war, both choices have backers with valid arguments and grievances. I use these terms commutably out of respect for both sides. The dresses and accessories encountered in this book were made for and were used by their creators and wearers as a part of daily life.

The stunning beauty of 19th century Plains Indian women's garments is not only a feast for the eyes, but is also both a testimony to the artistic abilities of the artists and a window to their souls. It is my hope that through this book you will gain a new appreciation for these historic clothing styles, be enabled to reproduce them with confidence, and then to wear them with the dignity and respect they are due.

This magnificent portrait of a handsome Sioux woman wearing her dentalium shell decorated, saved-list wool dress is classic in every respect. Replete with all accessories, her outfit includes a calico under dress, German silver concho belt and drag, bone hairpipe and bead breastplate, wide brass bracelets, ball and cone earrings, fully beaded moccasins, and a typical woolen shawl in plaid design. Photographer unknown; courtesy of Nebraska Historical Society. Photo Number RG2063-332.

ACKNOWLEDGEMENTS

I would like to extend my sincere appreciation to Earl and Faith Fenner and Benson Lanford, who spent many hours proofing, analyzing and editing the original manuscript, sketches and photographs. They provided numerous suggestions and insightful comments, unselfishly sharing their immense knowledge and skills, thus helping to make this work as historically accurate as possible, as well as making it a more practical reference for the craftsmen who will ultimately use it.

Special consideration is due Alex Koslov for his tremendous contribution of the many fine illustrations and sketches, and Wes Housler for his comments on mountain sheep hide dresses, finally correcting a long standing misconception regarding the use of deer and elk skin.

Acknowledgements are also gratefully extended to the following individuals and institutions who provided photographs, artwork, suggestions, and/or expertise: Heinz Bründl (Germany); Sam Cahoon; Allen Chronister; Shilice Clinkscales, National Museum of the American Indian; Mike Cowdrey; Richard Green (UK); Pat Hartless; Rick Hewitt; Bill Holm; Sylvia Inwood, The Detroit Institute of Arts; Maj. Gen. Michael C. Kostelnick, USAF (Ret.); Bob Laidig; Joe Rivera, Henry C. Monahan, and Lisa Delisi-Holmes, Morning Star Gallery; Mark Halverson and Sharon Silengo, State Historical Society of North Dakota; Jack Heriard, Written Heritage Publications; Joan Barnes, The Masco Corporation; Michael Martin, Flint Institute of Arts; Larry Mensching, Joslyn Art Museum; Richard Pohrt, Jr.; David L. Stuart; Roger Schustereit; Dan Swan, formerly of The Gilcrease Museum; Michael Terry, Mark Thiel, Marquette University; Robert Wagner, Hudson's Bay Indian Trading Post (Germany); and Bob Voelker.

Sincerest gratitude is extended to Rex, Ginger and Jessica Reddick, Bob Sanford, Andy Russell, Ed Wells and all the other folks at Crazy Crow Trading Post for their interest in and contributions to this project. It has been a privilege and a pleasure. Thanks also go to my husband, David, who is not only my best friend, but also a talented historian with a God-given gift for seeing the bigger picture. He has been a constant source of encouragement, space, literary criticism and wise counsel. And finally, I offer grateful tribute to the Creator who has been a constant source of strength on this most unusual of paths.

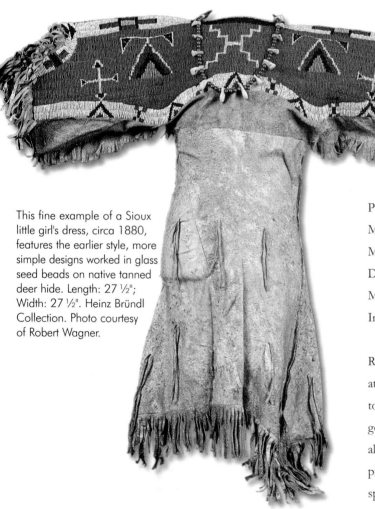

This fine example of a Sioux little girl's dress, circa 1880, features the earlier style, more simple designs worked in glass seed beads on native tanned deer hide. Length: 27 ½"; Width: 27 ½". Heinz Bründl Collection. Photo courtesy of Robert Wagner.

Chapter 1:
PLAINS DRESSES

In order to fully appreciate the fashions described in this book, it is important to understand the structure of four basic dress types used by Plains Indian women in the 19th Century: Sidefold, Two-Hide, Three-Hide, and the Tradecloth dress.

Chan-Cha-Nia-Teuin (Woman of the Crow Nation), Teton Sioux Woman

– Karl Bodmer watercolor
Painted on June1, 1833 at Ft. Pierre. This young woman's name implies a kinship with the Crow tribe, bitter enemies of the Sioux. It is possible that she may have been taken captive in a raid, and raised as a Sioux. She valued her dress too highly to sell it, but Prince Maximilian was able to purchase her buffalo robe and it now resides in Stuttgart, Germany. Note the decoration at the bottom of her dress and her moccasins and leggings.
Courtesy of the Joslyn Art Museum, Omaha, NE 1986.49.305

BASIC STYLES
Sidefold, Two-Hide, Three-Hide, and Tradecolth Dresses

The Sidefold Dress was constructed from a large, tanned animal skin, which was generally buffalo without the tail. When oriented with the tail end of the hide up and folded over so as to form the top of the dress, it was large enough to completely encase the wearer's body. This produced a garment with only one seam, typically up the left side of the wearer. The top of the hide is folded horizontally, producing 'a straight top edge' and a flap in front and back that typically 'hangs to about the waist' (Feder,1984:48). [If a large enough hide could not be found, two hides 'joined horizontally' might be used. In this case, the bottom of the flap fell 'down almost to the mid-seam' where the hides were connected (Conn, 1955:30)]. After folding the top down to produce the flap, a vertical slit was made in the folded edge of the hide. This formed the armhole for the wearer's right arm. A shoulder strap was 'sewn in place to fit over the right shoulder' (Feder, 1984:48). A neck-to-shoulder seam connected the front and back of the bodice over the left shoulder. Because of the way the dress was constructed, any leg extensions on the hide naturally fell at the bottom margin of the flap and the hemline of the finished garment.

Peabody Museum, Harvard University, from Photo No. T2926.
Illustration by Alex Koslov.

Example of a Sioux dress.

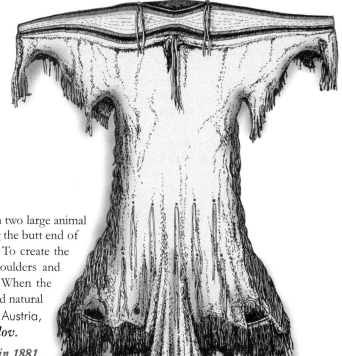

The Two-Hide or "Tail" Dress was made from two large animal skins tanned so as to leave a narrow edging of hair along the butt end of the hides, including the tail itself (Wissler, 1915: 99). To create the dress, two hides were joined by seams "along the shoulders and down the sides below the arms" (Conn, 1955:32-33). When the shoulder seam was sewn, the leg area of the hides formed natural cape-like sleeves. Museum für Volkerkunde, Vienna, Austria, from Catalog No. 13671. *Illustration by Alex Koslov.*

Example of a Crow(?) dress, acquired in 1881.

The Three-Hide Dress was constructed of three tanned animal hides, two of which made up the skirt, or lower section of the garment. The third hide was folded lengthwise (head to tail), centered over the skirt, and then sewn securely to it, front and back, although some groups did not join the yoke. This third hide formed the upper section, or cape-like yoke, of the garment (Conn, 1955:36). The head and tail ends of this hide became the sleeves. Sometimes, the leg extensions on the hides were left intact and were retained just as they fell, as additional decorations." Morning Star Gallery.

Illustration by Alex Koslov.
Example of a Cheyenne dress.

The Tradecloth Dress was structurally similar to earlier hide dresses, from which it's distinct form developed. The tradecloth dress was made out of garment-weight Euro-American-made woolen or cotton yard goods. Two large pieces usually formed the front and back of the dress, and two smaller pieces produced the sleeves. Tribal distinctives include triangular side gussets, a contrasting color triangular, cloth decorative addition around the neck opening, and decorative devices such as elk teeth, shells or coins.

The Crow woman's trade wool dress shown at right was collected by William Wildschut, ca. 1923, and is decorated with beadwork and imitation elk teeth carved from bone. National Museum of the American Indian, from Catalog No. 12/6406. *Illustration by Alex Koslov.*
Example of a Crow dress.

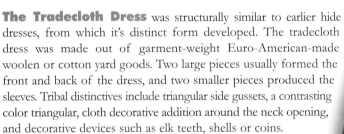

Chapter 1: Basic Dress Styles

With a few minor variations dependent on tribal and personal stylization, these four dress types are the basis for most Plains Indian women's garments during the early-to-mid 1800s. Even the cloth dresses we will encounter in this brief study have their structural basis in earlier hide dress examples. Familiarity with these dress types is essential to the crafter who wishes to successfully recreate them.

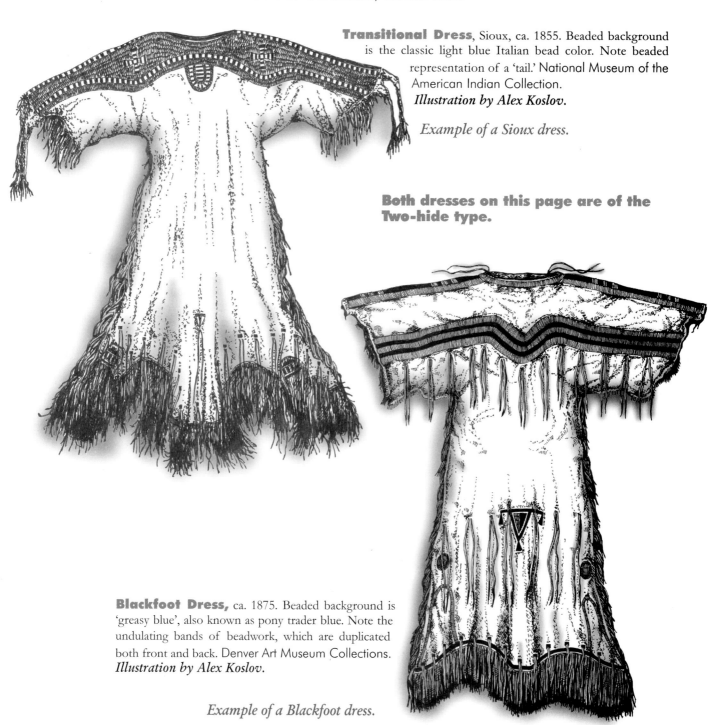

Transitional Dress, Sioux, ca. 1855. Beaded background is the classic light blue Italian bead color. Note beaded representation of a 'tail.' National Museum of the American Indian Collection. *Illustration by Alex Koslov.*

Example of a Sioux dress.

Both dresses on this page are of the Two-hide type.

Blackfoot Dress, ca. 1875. Beaded background is 'greasy blue', also known as pony trader blue. Note the undulating bands of beadwork, which are duplicated both front and back. Denver Art Museum Collections. *Illustration by Alex Koslov.*

Example of a Blackfoot dress.

WOMEN'S ACCESSORIES
During the 19th Century

Besides the dress itself, there were four additional basic wardrobe items for the historic Plains Indian Woman; moccasins, leggings, a belt, and a robe. Later, with the introduction of cloth as a trade item, a simple piece of cloth similar to an apron was wrapped around the waist, and was especially popular among Southern Plains tribes, along with a military officer's style wool fringed sash. Moccasins were the universal footwear of the Plains tribes. Leggings were "worn by all Plains women — it was considered improper to appear without them" (Conn, 1982:143). However, Southern Plains tribes often wore high top moccasins, which incorporated the legging with the moccasin, while others wore moccasins with ankle extensions for everyday wear. The belt was a necessary carry-all for the woman's tools. A robe (or other cloak) not only protected the wearer from inclement weather, but in many tribes was worn out of social propriety.

Moccasins, leggings, a belt and a hide robe, wool blanket or shawl should be considered essential to re-creating the total historic look at rendezvous or pow wow. They should be made with as much care and attention to detail as the primary garment. Nothing can spoil the impression of even the most beautiful "repro" dress faster than the use of inappropriate (wrong tribe/time period) or poorly made accessories.

There are several good resources available which can walk you through the making of these additional items. For moccasin and legging ideas consult: White, 1969; Johnson, 1996; Conn, 1989; and Full Circle Communications, 1997.

Basic comments about belts and robes can be found in numerous publications, including: Koch, 1977, Jennys, 1993 (2) and Fecteau, 1979. Useful information about belts is "patchy" and widely scattered, but with a little diligence the crafter can assemble enough material to facilitate correct interpretation.

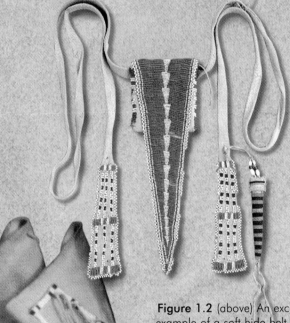

Figure 1.2 (above) An excellent example of a soft-hide belt in the traditional Sioux style. Note the exaggerated flap on the pouch, the addition of a quill-decorated awl case, and the flared, beaded end tabs of the belt. Private collection.

Figure 1.3 Author's re-creation of Upper Missouri style moccasins and leggings dating to the first half of the 19th century. Made from elk hide and adorned with size 8/0 pony beads in three hues of blue and white. Photo by the author.

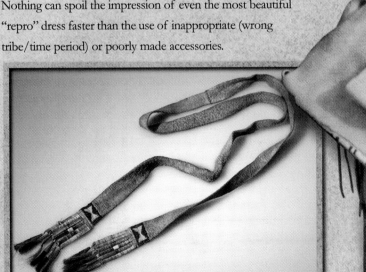

Figure 1.1 Sioux quill decorated buckskin belt. Photo courtesy of American Museum of Natural History, [50.214445].

Chapter 1: Basic Dress Styles

5

GENERAL CONSTRUCTION TECHNIQUES

MATERIAL CONSIDERATIONS

A friend once told me a finished garment is only as good as its materials. This statement is probably nowhere as true as it is with Plains Indian hide dresses. You cannot start with poor quality materials and expect to achieve high quality results! Selecting just the right hides for a leather dress is a very important first step in the construction process. Elk and deer leather are the optimal choices for the best finished look. I strongly suggest that crafters steer clear of leather "alternative" fabrics such as "ultra-suede"® and "naugahyde"®. Sueded cowhide is often the least expensive "genuine leather" material available for making garments, and if sueded on both sides will produce a garment with a look similar to elk or deer. Thus, it is always preferable to wait for those "perfect" materials, rather than going ahead with second-best. Elk or deer is definitely preferred. Don't rush a project, and in doing so sacrifice its beauty or historical integrity. John C. Ewers once wrote that Blackfeet women "are quick to notice and approve a finely dressed skin of soft, even texture and color, or a well-made skin article. They are quick to reject a poorly dressed skin or a careless piece of sewing" (Ewers, 1945:14).

The best way to be sure to get exactly the leather you need is to purchase it in person. This allows you to hand-pick the hides yourself. Leather can be purchased at most larger powwows and rendezvous, and in leather craft stores around the country. If purchasing hides in person is not possible, the next best thing for most folks is to purchase via mail order. There are numerous businesses that cater to pow wow and living history needs, and some have extensive catalogs with many different leather choices. Before purchasing, request "samples" of the leather so you know what you're getting. Telephone a sales representative and discuss your project, explaining to them exactly what you need to complete it. In most cases they will be happy to select hides in accordance with the information you have given them.

Generally speaking, the larger the frame of the intended wearer, the larger the hides required for a garment's construction. A woman of medium build should expect to need hides with at least 12-14 square feet of blemish-free surface per hide. Often this means beginning with elk hides or large deer hides! Smaller deer hides are better suited for a child's dress. Each hide should be long enough from head end to butt end to hang from the wearer's shoulder to below the middle of her calf. Be sure to add enough to the length measurement, beginning at the mid top of the shoulder, to allow for the bust and the amount of leather or cloth that will be taken up by the addition of a belt.

An important feature to keep in mind is that Indian dresses should not fit the body snugly, but should have ample material that is gathered at the wearer's sides. Furthermore, long slits up the sides of the skirt are definitely not an Indian feature either. The fullness of the skirt permits freedom of movement.

Whatever the project, it is always prudent to purchase more buckskin than you think you will need. This is extremely important if you also wish to make accessories that match in hide finish and color. Being skimpy with leather can result in a finished dress that will turn heads at the local rendezvous, but will not pass the historical test of "can she butcher a bison, tan hides, and ride horseback?" and still be comfortable and acceptably modest.

It is important to note that not all garments were made from the largest hides and were not always perfect. Indians pieced and recycled all the time and the results were often quite striking, so keep in mind that there is nothing wrong with piecing hides together to make an item rather than spending a great deal for the largest hides one can find. This is especially true when the hide being pieced was eventually to be covered with beadwork. An excellent example of this is the beautiful Blood dress illustrated on page 18, Fig. 2.16.

> When assembling hides for the construction of dresses, the shape of the hides is of paramount importance.

BRAIN-TANNED OR COMMERCIALLY-TANNED?

There are basically three different types of leather available to the crafter: brain-tanned, also known as Indian-tanned, commercial-tanned, and German-tanned. Unless you have the know-how and experience to brain tan your own hides, you are left with the alternative of purchasing one of the three types. Brain-tanned hides are quite expensive - usually from $12 to $20 per square foot! These prices can create an expensive endeavor, particularly when trying to outfit an entire family for rendezvous or powwow. Hence for the average crafter or buckskinner, commercial or German-tanned hides are the most cost-effective alternative to brain-tanned. Relatively new to the U.S. market, German-tanned buckskin is similarly priced to commercial-tanned and is available in white, smoked, and natural colors. It is sueded on both sides like brain-tan and is found in the larger sizes required for dresses. It is difficult to distinguish from brain-tanned in texture and working characteristics, being much easier to sew and bead on; however, the white color can become discolored when wet, but can be dyed or painted with powder paints.

It has been argued that only the use of brain-tanned hides guarantees the "authenticity" of a finished garment, but there are often "holes" in these arguments. I have encountered crafters who disdain the use of commercial leather as un-authentic yet recommend the synthetic "nymo" as a thread medium! Unless you are involved in very specific jobs/situations requiring absolute exact reproduction of Plains Indian material culture, right down to antique beads and sinew sewing, you may consider commercially-tanned hides an option to brain-tanned ones.

Whether brain-tanned or commercially-tanned, before you use any hide, it must meet certain criteria, one of which is shape. When assembling hides for the construction of dresses, the shape of the hides is of paramount importance. Each hide selected should look like it was taken from the animal with care. A decent quality commercially-tanned hide will have to be trimmed to pass the "shape" test, so that it will look roughly like the outline shown in Figure 1.4. If you are using brain-tanned hides you increase the chance of having hides that look right and even retain the tail and an edging of hair along the butt end. With commercial hides, it will be necessary in most cases to physically recreate their shape by "artificial" means. Too much trimming can reduce the useable size of the hides, perhaps necessitating the construction of a Type 2 or Type 3 garment rather than a Type 1 (See page 13). The shape of a hide determines its usefulness for a project.

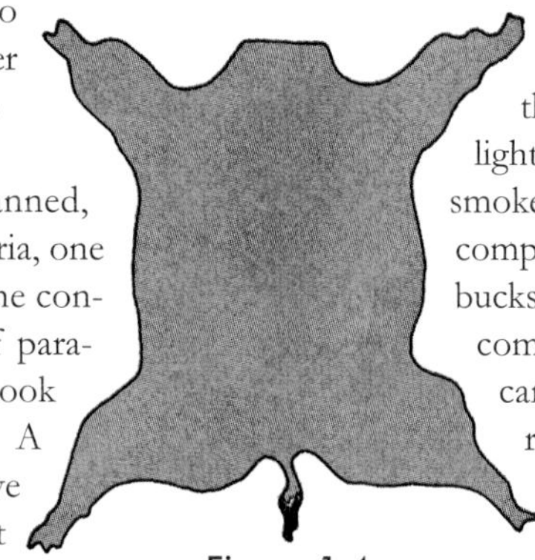

Another useful criteria is the hide's texture. Brain-tanned and German-tanned hides have a soft roughened texture on both sides. Most commercial skins have two textures, one side of the hide is "rough" and one side is "slick"; however, some commercial hides are sueded on both sides. Many of the garments you will see at rendezvous and powwows have been constructed with the slick side out (visible). I personally prefer to keep the slick side in because the rough side looks more like the texture of brain-tanned. Turning the slick side in will cause the garment to stick to your skin, but here's a word of advice: Mount a stretching/breaking rope as shown in Figure 1.5 and give the slick side of the hides a thorough rubbing. "Roughing" the slick side does not alter the texture enough to negate using the rough side out, but with a little old-fashioned elbow grease, much of the shiny slickness can be eliminated, making the hides a bit more comfortable next to the skin. Keep in mind, however, that all buckskin will stick to a sweaty body. An authentic way to cope with this is to wear a light underdress of cotton.

The color of the leather is also an important factor to consider. Remember that shades of creamy tan and tawny brown are reminiscent of colors achieved by the historic process of smoking a brain-tanned hide. If the garment is to look right, bizarre leather colors must be avoided, particularly the bright oranges, reds, and "biker black". For authenticity, stick to a natural buckskin color that is historically appropriate. If you buy commercial leather in any shade except white, purchase all you will need from one source at the same time. Hide colors run in "lots" just like bead colors and re-matching is next to impossible.

Figure 1.4

When deciding whether to use white or smoke-tan colored leather in your garment construction, you must think first about how you will be using the finished item. Historically, white buckskin dresses with elaborate decoration were reserved for very special occasions, and most of these were probably not pure white, having at least a light smoking. Workaday garments were made from smoked hides that better hid dirt and smudges. It may be completely appropriate for you to wear a beautiful white buckskin dress into the dance arena at a powwow, but completely inappropriate to wear such a dress while carrying out messy camp chores at a living history rendezvous. Non-white hides are the more practical choice for most rendezvous needs. Save the pure whites for dress-up!

A little "trick" you can use to simulate a brain-tanned look from commercially-tanned leather is to buy light colored hides in shades of white and smoke them yourself as if you had just finished tanning them, although it can be quite difficult to get them to accept the smoke color. There are plenty of decent instructions available that can walk you through the smoking process and with a little practice you will get beautiful woodsy tones that will significantly aide in the overall appearance of a finished garment. There is also an added bonus to smoking

Figure 1.5 Mount a stretching / breaking rope and add elbow grease to "rough up" the slick side of buckskin to enhance wearing comfort of garment.

Chapter 1: Basic Dress Styles

commercial leather, and this is the elimination of that pungent "factory" or mothball odor! The leather can also be colored by rubbing it all over with powdered pigment of the appropriated color (such as a good shade of ochre as seen on the dress in Figure 5.1 on page 75) and then dampening it with water and rubbing the pigment to set it.

Be sure your hides are ready for use before beginning the construction process. This includes patching all holes. Here's how: Round out any jagged holes. Use the outline of the hole to determine the size of the patch — which should be exactly the same size as the hole. Cut the patch from a remote edge of the leather and remember to match surface textures. While holding the patch in place, use a needle and fine thread and — from the back side of the hide — with a whip stitch attach the patch completely around the inside of the hole and shown in Figure 1.6. Be careful to keep the stitches small and as invisible as possible from the front side. When finished, take several back stitches and tie the end of the thread off. Flatten the seam by pounding with a mallet.

Besides the leather, the crafter will need these items to make a basic dress: scissors, sewing awl, glovers needles, thread medium (artificial sinew is recommended for hide garments; linen quilter's thread for trade cloth garments) tape measure, yard stick and ruler and a fabric marker. Depending on the garment you may also need trade wool for necklines and accents on a leather dress,

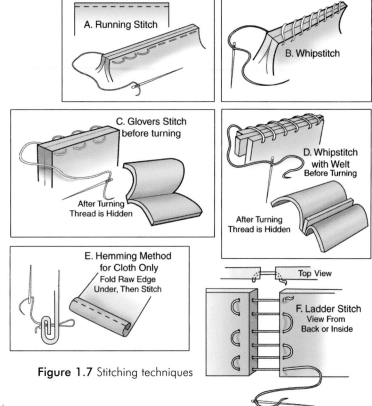

Figure 1.7 Stitching techniques

or for the body of a cloth one, a contrasting color trade wool for the yoke, cuff, and hem of a Crow-style dress, cotton cloth if you wish to line a trade wool garment, and ribbon. Your work surface should be large, flat and well-lit.

STITCHING & HEMMING TIPS

Use a ½" seam allowance on cloth garments unless otherwise specified, and ¼" or less on leather. If you are using a sewing machine, the throat plate should be marked for a ½" seam. If it is not, you can mark it yourself with a strip of adhesive tape. When sewing leather by hand, we recommend using an awl and regular needle. Glover's needles have a sharp triangular point that makes piercing leather easier, but leave larger holes which can elongate under pressure. If you use them, watch the triangular edges as they are very sharp! When hemming cloth garments, turn edges under and fold again so that no raw edges are exposed. See Figure 1.7E

LADDER STITCH

This stitch is very handy for sewing leather together with a flat junction, and is especially useful for piecing hides when necessary as the stitching is visible only on the reverse side.

Sew leather through the edges, coming out on the back side or wrong side. Push the needle through the back side of the leather, coming out on the edge. Enter the second piece of leather on the edge, coming out on the back side. Move ¼" to ³/₈" to insert needle in back of second piece and repeat procedure coming out on back side of first piece. Continue sewing until seam is finished. Fasten and cut thread. See Fig. 1.7F.

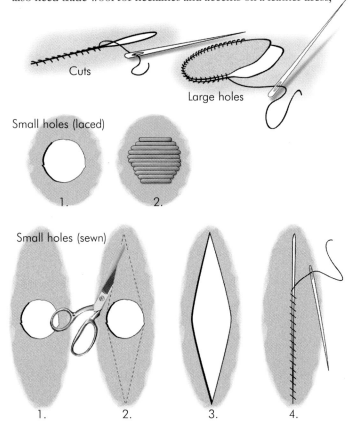

Figure 1.6 Four traditional and effective techniques used to patch holes and cuts in buckskin.

19th Century Plains Indian Dresses

Chapter 2:
NORTHERN PLAINS

The Northern Plains is the homeland of the Blackfoot/Blackfeet, Gros Ventres, Assiniboine and Stoney, Sarsi, Hidatsa, Arikara, Crow, Mandan, Plains Cree and Plains Ojibwe/Bungi/Saulteau peoples, to name a few. It is a region of contrasts: rolling grassland and rugged mountains and powerful rivers; a region of unbelievable temperature swings and bitter cold winters. Historic women's clothing styles among the Northern Plains tribes were also diverse. One of the most distinctive tribal dress styles was that of the the Crow, while the Blackfoot dress was very close to that of the Plateau tribes.

Dress, ca. 1830-50, Upper Missouri region, Montana or North Dakota. This classic hide dress is decorated with pony beads in blue, black and white, hawk bells, red cloth, and buckskin fringe. Length 54¾", width 49". Collection of Flint Institute of Arts; Dirk Bakker, Photographer. Photograph ©1992, The Detroit Institute of Arts.

BLACKFOOT STYLE: Two-Hide Dress

The oldest significant source of written information about Blackfoot garments is the journal of David Thompson, ca. 1784 (Thompson 1916). His notes on women's attire clearly describe a strap dress with separate sleeves as being a primary fashion during this time. Undoubtedly, this is a carry-over from the general Woodlands and Algonkian style, and was not necessarily limited to the Blackfoot.

Apparently this style remained fashionable well into the next century, because Daniel Harmon's ca. 1810 journal also mentions it. Whether the strap dress was just one of several garment-types being worn by Blackfoot women during this time frame is unclear. What we do know is that at the time Prince Maximilian visited the Plains almost twenty-five years later, Blackfoot women were wearing the two-hide dress style almost exclusively. However, it is highly probable that both styles were worn concurrently even if the latter was more popular.

> **Beadwork on old Blackfoot dresses is primarily an aestheic accent which compliments the simple beauty of the hides themselves, as well as the outline of the bottom of the hide and the yoke.**

Maximilian's journal of 1832-1834 (Maximilian, 1906) describes the two-hide dresses as having short wide sleeves and a hemline both fringed and scalloped. Ornamentation included quillwork on the hem and sleeves (quillwork being an old form of applied decoration), lanes of sky-blue and white beadwork, and rows of elk teeth or buttons.

According to the authors of The Blackfoot Craftworker's Book, the typical old style Blackfoot two-skin dress was made by orienting the hides head down. The neck and foreleg contours were left intact (Hungry Wolf, 1977:42). This gave the hemline a unique shape: two side flaps and a central pendant area, separated by crescent curves. If the hides to be used in the creation of a dress did not have the desired look, they might be cut and/or pieced to achieve it. "Close examination shows that most dresses have pieces of skin added in various places to fill out the hides" (Ibid: 42). These created contours still were said to represent the animals whose hide formed the dress (Schneider 1968:14). However, this is not to say they represented specific animal skins per se.

Figure 2.1 Blackfoot, ca. 1830. Author's interpretation of an Upper Missouri style dress from the first half of the 19th century. Dress was made from..commercially tanned buckskin using the techniques described in this book. Photo by Susan Jennys.

Karl Bodmer's rendering, "Piegan Blackfeet Woman," shown on the cover, beautifully illustrates the historic Blackfoot two-hide dress. Because she is rather stooped the dress is shortened somewhat. When standing straight, it should reach at least to mid-calf. It is adorned with a single row of light blue and white lane stitch beadwork covering the neck-to-wrist seam, leather pendant thongs attached parallel to the bottom of the yoke and these are strung with large beads, more leather pendant thongs, anchoring fabric snippets attached parallel to the hemline, small rectangles of fabric inset into the hemline, and a triangular fabric ornament sewn to the lower middle of the skirt portion. These fabric patches were "generally made of trade cloth and divided in half by color, with one side red and the other black or dark blue" (Hungry Wolf, 1977:43). They were often edged with beads and/or a narrow lane of buckskin. Some Blackfoot craftworkers have said that the two rectangular fabric patches "represent the kidneys, though their original meanings may be lost" (Ibid: 42). The triangular ornament is an ancient symbol said to be associated with womanhood (Ibid: 42).

Beadwork on old Blackfoot dresses is primarily an aesthetic accent which compliments the simple beauty of the hides themselves, as well as the outline of the bottom of the hide and the yoke. The beadwork on mid-to-late 19th century dresses was more elaborate and included a wide band of parallel lane stitch rows running horizontally across the upper area of the dress in front and back. Beadwork was executed in pony beads — or real beads, as craftworkers called them. Today they are more commonly known as pony beads. Typically two contrasting bead colors, such as blue and white or black and white, were used in the bands. This created a pleasing horizontal stripe effect. The beaded lanes were often arranged so that light color lanes were on the "outside" or top and bottom of the band. "Sometimes the colored stripes were broken up with small geometric sections, but rarely with any other designs" (Ibid: 42-43).

The front and back of the dress was virtually always identical. Beaded bands in lane stitch were identically applied on the front and back of the dress. A single lane of beadwork following the contours of the hemline was also a popular and elegant adornment technique. "In the old days wealthy men's wives were wont to decorate their dresses with one or more rows of elk teeth instead of, or in addition to, the beadwork" (Ewers, 1945:44).

CONSTRUCTION

When assembling hides for construction of the Blackfoot-style two-hide dress, the shape of the hides is of paramount importance. If you use brain-tanned hides you increase the chance of having hides that look right and even retain the tail and an edging of hair along the butt end.

If you use commercially tanned hides which usually have a "slick" grain side, it will be necessary in most cases to physically re-create the hides' shape by approximating the natural contour by carefully cutting it. Too much trimming can reduce the useable size of the

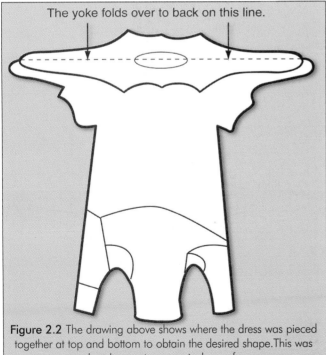

Figure 2.2 The drawing above shows where the dress was pieced together at top and bottom to obtain the desired shape. This was not unusual and a most economical use of a resource.

The yoke folds over to back on this line.

hides, perhaps necessitating the construction of a Type 2 or Type 3 garment rather than a Type 1. Generally speaking, if you wish to create a Type 1 garment for an adult, you should begin with two large elk hides. Two good-sized deer hides will usually make a child's dress.

Here are a few more tips: Double check all measurements. It is always better to err on the side of caution. If your garment turns out slightly too large...no problem! Just belt it. If it's too small, long triangular gussets can be added into the side seams — but this is a lot of extra work, though historically correct in construction.

Keep your stitches small and tight. While you do not want your seams to be too tight so that they pucker, you do want them tight enough to be neat and secure. Pulling stitches too tightly can also cause the seam to roll. Double tie all knots, and reinforce all stress points (at the ends of the neck opening, under the arm pits, at the bottom of the side seams, etc.). This can help reduce future ravelings and pull-outs.

For piercing holes, use a round-shaped awl rather than a wedge-shaped one. Wedge or "Glovers" shaped awls will make a nasty jagged tear rather than a clean, round hole and tears will rip out much faster. DO NOT USE A LEATHER PUNCH, as it removes material while the awl displaces material which will naturally fill back in.

Be patient and WAIT for those "perfect" materials, rather than going ahead with inferior materials. TAKE YOUR TIME —don't rush to complete a project and sacrifice the beauty and integrity of the finished garment. You want to create a garmet you can be proud to wear! The actual making of the two-hide dress is relatively simple. As mentioned earlier, the two hides must be large enough to form the entire front and back of the dress — plus plenty of extra! Mountain sheep hides were the most widely preferred, as they are large and tough. However, the purchase of elk hides might be required to obtain the necessary amount of leather for larger-framed women. In most cases, getting two more-than-adequately sized elk hides will cost far less in both money and time than four deer hides of the same square footage.

THE SHOULDER UPPER BODICE

Lay the two hides together, rough sides facing each other, in order to simulate brain-tanned buckskin. Match the shape, end-for-end; the larger, butt end of the hides will form the top of the dress. The two-hide dress usually has a classic "yoke". With brain-tanned or German-tanned hides, this yoke is achieved by sewing across the shoulder line about six inches from the top of the hide, then flipping the excess or each hide down front and back, and tacking it in place. The basic idea is to obtain the correct length dress for the person for whom it is being constructed, and to supply an even line or seam along the top of the shoulders. If you are using commercially tanned hides you will need to use a "cut and flip" or a "modified cut and flip" method to maintain the continuity of the hide texture as you create the yoke area of your dress.

Using the method of cutting, flipping and then tacking the bottom of the yoke in place on the top of the dress body or the "skirt", automatically turns the smooth side inward on commerical hides.

In the basic "cut and flip" method, the hides are cut horizontally across the shoulder line about six inches below the top of mid-center. The width of this yoke piece is critical in determining the length of the finished dress. If the hides you are using are large enough that the total length of the leather, minus the removed piece for the yoke, will comfortably and modestly cover the intended wearer from shoulder to lower-calf, (check length) you can proceed with the attachment of the yoke to the bodice. Both halves are sewn together, outside in, bodice to bodice, yoke to yoke, leaving a ¼" seam allowance and a ten-inch neck opening in the center of both the yoke and bodice. By sewing the pieces together outside in, the correct side will show when the leather is turned right side out.

Spread out the dress piece as shown in Figure 2.4. Lay the yoke on it as shown and align the two long seams, rough side up. Fasten the yoke to the dress with decorative thongs along the

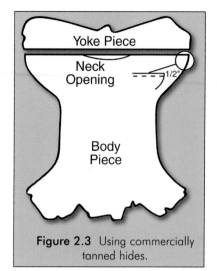

Figure 2.3 Using commercially tanned hides.

bottom edges, front and back. This should be done carefully, using the same number of thongs on the back as on the front. Space them evenly across the yoke and leave several inches between each one.

The neck openings should match up. Attach them to each other by using a binding of blue or red wool trade cloth approximately 2" x 22". If wool cloth is chosen, the color should be complimentary to the dress, yet in keeping with colors historically available (see chapter on Sioux Tradecloth dresses for more information). The binding is usually held in place with a very wide spiraling whipstitch using a thin thong which provides additional decoration. If done with sinew it would normally be finely stitched so as to hide the sinew as much as possible. Note however, that many older style dresses have no neck binding at all.

After tacking the yoke in place over the bodice with thong fringe and neck binding, pick up the garment at the shoulder seam and hold it up. You should now have a two-hide, yoked dress with two layers of leather at the yoke, and only the rough textured sides of the commercial leather showing (Figure 2.8).

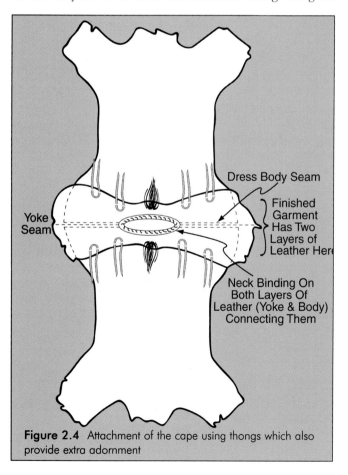

Figure 2.4 Attachment of the cape using thongs which also provide extra adornment

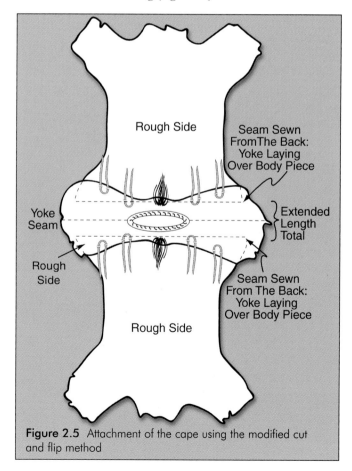

Figure 2.5 Attachment of the cape using the modified cut and flip method

THE TWO HIDE DRESS:
A Closer Look

The two-hide dress style is probably an ancient one. Although it has been said that the slip-and-sleeve and sidefold dress styles were its antecedent, probably at one point in time the three styles were concurrent, with the sidefold fading out of fashion sooner, while the slip-and-sleeve remained in use longer among numbers of people, as the two-hide style came in. The two-hide dress can be comfortably documented to the early 1800s. It was used by such Northern, Central Plains, and Plateau tribes as the Blackfoot, Crow, Assiniboine, Dakota, Mandan, Hidatsa, Nez Perce, Yakima, and Flathead, among others (Conn, 1955:33).

In his study, "Structural Basis to the Decoration of Costumes Among the Plains Indians", Clark Wissler described three distinct variations or sub-types of the two-hide dress, defined by the manner in which the yoke of the garment was constructed. In Type 1, the butt end of the two hides that form the top of the dress are sewn together several inches from the edge. The bulk of the hides forms the body of the dress. The remainder above the seam, two narrow strips with retained tail and hair along the edge, are simply folded down and secured over the bodice (top portion of the dress) in front and back. This folded over yoke with tail produces a unique undulating contour of double thickness that "defines a peculiar curve whose origin is in the original material and not in the aesthetic constructive activities of the maker" (Wissler, 1916:99).

Type 2 of the two-hide dress variations is created in a slightly different manner but produces the same visual result. A bit more stitching is required for this technique. As with Type 1, two hides are connected vertically by a seam across the top. The excess narrow strips are removed (instead of a folding them down to form a yoke). A separate yoke is created by using the tail ends of two additional

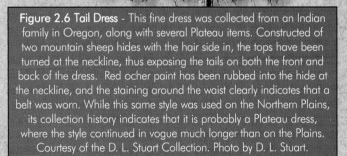

Figure 2.6 Tail Dress - This fine dress was collected from an Indian family in Oregon, along with several Plateau items. Constructed of two mountain sheep hides with the hair side in, the tops have been turned at the neckline, thus exposing the tails on both the front and back of the dress. Red ocher paint has been rubbed into the hide at the neckline, and the staining around the waist clearly indicates that a belt was worn. While this same style was used on the Northern Plains, its collection history indicates that it is probably a Plateau dress, where the style continued in vogue much longer than on the Plains. Courtesy of the D. L. Stuart Collection. Photo by D. L. Stuart.

hides joined together by a long seam (interrupted only for a neck opening). By carefully sewing this yoke onto the dress, the finished garment had the same tail tuft and curved yoke look as Type 1. This variation required considerably more stitching and was probably used if the two hides for the dress were either not large enough to facilitate both the bodice and the folded yoke, or when the hides did not have quite the requisite tail-and-contour shape.

The Type 3 two-hide dress is technically a three-hide dress! Wissler assigned this sub-type to those older Lakota dresses with significant beadwork, usually executed in pony beads on the bodices. Rather than a narrow self-yoke, the Type 3 garment has a wide rectangular shaped yoke made out of a portion of a separate hide.

This yoke is attached to the skirt section of the dress (formed of two hides) by straight horizontal seams in front and back. Due to the semi-tailored shape and size of the yoke, the natural hide contour is minimized and there is no tail tuft. Rather, the layout of beaded lanes is carefully planned so that the rows (in lane stitch) imitate the contours of the tail end of the hide as if it were present, requiring gently undulating lanes with a small sharp downward curve in the middle (Ibid:101). A broad beaded band often parallels the contoured lane(s). Fully beaded yokes on dresses of this style are rare. Most are "only partially beaded, as shown by Bodmer and Catlin" (Lessard, 1980:71). The replacement of the actual tail with a beaded u-shape was a mid-19th Century Dakota stylistic development. It persists as a common design element on the fully (seed) beaded yokes of late 19th century dresses and continues on traditional dresses to the present.

Of the four dress styles presented in this book, the two-hide is the simplest one for the beginning crafter to reproduce with success.

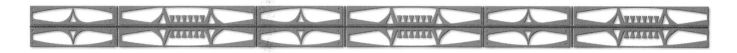

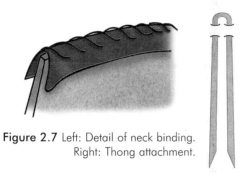

Figure 2.7 Left: Detail of neck binding.
Right: Thong attachment.

MODIFIED CUT-AND-FLIP METHOD

If the hides are not quite long enough without the removed yoke piece to comfortably and modestly cover the intended wearer from shoulder to mid-calf, (check length) you can extend the length a bit by using the yoke piece as the very top of the finished dress, rather than as an overlaid piece. This method can add almost six inches to the total length. Here is how to proceed:

Put the two yoke pieces on top of each other with the rough sides facing each other. Sew them together along the straight side ("yoke seam", Figure 2.5) using a very fine overcast or oblique whip stitch. Don't forget to leave an unsewn ten-inch neck opening in the center! Spread out the three pieces (front, back and yoke) as shown in Figure 2.5. Lay the yoke carefully over on top of the bodice pieces, as illustrated. Remember to keep the rough texture of all pieces up. Align the pieces as shown, with the bottom center of the yoke piece overlaying the bodice pieces by no more than a half-inch! Mark and/or pin the yoke to the bodice pieces.

With the dress inside out, using a very fine running stitch, attach the yoke to the bodice pieces, one side at a time. Keep your stitches tight and check them on the front side regularly to make sure they appear uniform and the thread hasn't gotten bunched. The smaller and more uniform your stitches, the better the look of the finished garment. After the yoke is attached to both bodice pieces, turn the dress right side out and lay the leather out as in Figure 2.8. Fasten the "excess" bottom edges of the yoke to the bodice with thong fringes as shown. Space these thongs evenly. Proceed with attachment of a neck binding if desired. After this is complete, pick up the garment at the shoulders and hold it up. You should have a basic two-hide style garment, with the yoke area being a single layer of leather, and all rough-textured sides should be "out".

To simulate the old-style two-hide mountain sheep dress with the tail of the animal still in place on the turned-down yoke, a small deer tail taken from a tanned robe, preferably from a black-tailed deer, can be fastened to the lower center edge of the yoke, front and back. Adding the "tail" not only gives the finished dress a closer historic look, it also provides a visual aid for centering other decorations on the upper bodice. Any tail added to the yoke should be from the top layer only, small in size, with hair trimmed short to resemble that of a mountain sheep, and tacked down well enough so as not to stick up or outward from the garment. For detailed views see the dresses in Figures 2.1, 2.6, 2.14, 2.15, 3.17, 3.18 and 3.21.

CHOOSING SIDES

After the shoulder and yoke are completed, the side seams are the next step. Determining the location of these seams is done by donning the dress as thus far completed, outside out, with the shoulder seams lying flat on the shoulders and arms raised at a 90° angle from the sides. A friend — or spouse! — should be enlisted to pin the side seams together at several points; the arm pit (begin a hand's width down - important for getting the dress on and off), and at the waist, hip and thigh. Pin or otherwise mark no less than four separate points on each side to assure the fit will be comfortable, neither too tight, nor too bulky.

Lay the dress flat and with a single flowing line, using a yard stick if necessary, mark off the seams on both sides, front and back. Use the pinned places as guides for your seam, leaving a half-inch allowance (See Figure 2.5).

The excess hide is left in place and will become the "self-fringe" along the side of the dress after sewing -- another reason for starting with over-sized hides!

The sides should be lace-sewn, right side out, using a running stitch. Sew from the arm pit mark to within six inches of the bottom.

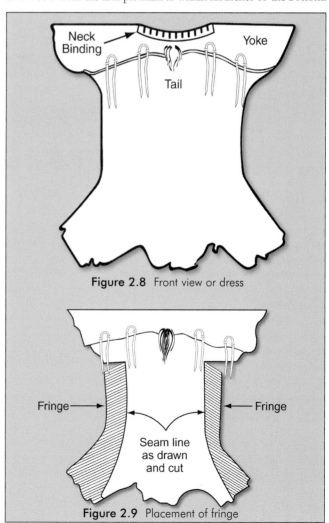

Figure 2.8 Front view or dress

Figure 2.9 Placement of fringe

A sharp awl will probably be necessary to pierce holes large enough for the lace to go through. Keep the running stitches as fine as possible. To be sure the side seams are sewn securely, tug gently at various spots down the seam on both sides of the dress.

After sewing is completed, cut the fringe pieces to within a half-inch of the finished seam, as shown in Figure 2.11. Length of the fringe is not nearly so important to the overall effect of the garment as the width of the individual strands. "Fat" fringe should be avoided. For best results, the strands should be no wider than ⅛". Cutting decent looking buckskin fringe takes lots of practice, but here is the best way. Cut the fringes fine and taper them to a point rather than a wide, blunt cut. After cutting, fringes should be dampened and pulled to separate them from each other and to get the "stretch" out of them -- in this way, they become finer and hang better.

GETTING TO THE BOTTOM

Historical dresses of the early 19th century were not cut straight off across the bottom and fringed! One need only consult the artwork of Catlin and Bodmer to note this fact. The shape of the bottom of the dress is determined by the hide's own form. The natural look of the hide as it has been taken from the neck/shoulder area of the animal was often preserved. Sometimes this uniquely contoured hemline was enhanced by the addition of minor fringing and rectangular leather or colored wool plugs.

Often a single row of beadwork ran parallel to these contours. (See Figures 2.12 and 2.13 on this page and additional photos in this section.) It is just as important to do a good job on the bottom of the dress as it is the top. This gives the garment a more "balanced" look.

Figure 2.10 Eva Sun Goes Slow, a girl of the Crow tribe with a type 2 skin dress and panel belt. Illustration from a photograph by Alex Koslov.

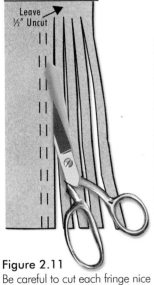

Figure 2.11
Be careful to cut each fringe nice and straight, an not "gig" it when cutting with scissors. Another excellent method is to cut it on a board with a sharp knife.

Cut Edge

Leave ½" Uncut

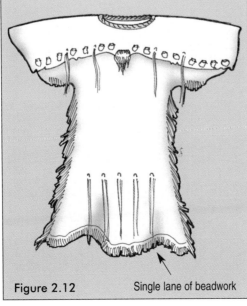

Figure 2.12 Single lane of beadwork

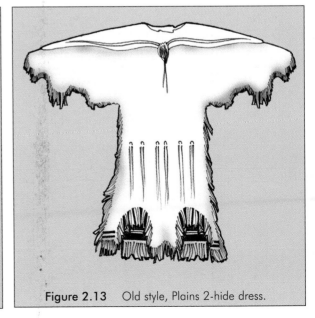

Figure 2.13 Old style, Plains 2-hide dress.

19th Century Plains Indian Dresses

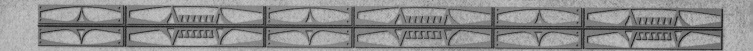

Figure 2.14. A Type-3 Two-Hide Dress attributed to the Piegan Blackfoot; however, this could possibly be an early Sioux dress as the beaded yoke reflects a definite Sioux influence. National Museum of the American Indian Collections.

19th Century Plains Indian Dresses

Front View

Side View

Figure 2.15 Blackfoot Dress, ca. 1835 - This classic, Type 1, Two-Skin dress is made from big horn sheep hides and features an undulating yoke, and decorated only with the tail of the animal and the strip of trimmed hair left around the edge of the hide. Note the typical red and black wool plugs which appear in the hemline contours on each side of the dress, both front and back. Coe Collection, Plains Indian Museum, Buffalo Bill Historical Center, Cody Wyoming, #202.376. Photo by the author.

Figure 2.16 This magnificent dress was collected from Little Ears, of the Blood Tribe, in Alberta Canada in the 1890's. Yoke features characteristic Blackfoot-style beadwork, in lane stitch, with additional lane stitch decoration to the skirt. Upon close examination, it is interesting to note that it is constructed of five or six hides, as it is heavily pieced, including a gusset on both sides. This is an excellent example of the result of Indians' ability to fully utilize their resources to great advantage, with very pleasing results. Height: 120cm (47.2 in.) Photo courtesy of the British Museum, London. Catalog No. 1903-31.

BLACKFOOT Accessories

cross the Plains and Plateau, the side-seam moccasin was the prevalent type - on the former until the mid-19th Century, the latter to the present day. The side seam is the oldest moccasin type in Blackfoot recollection, and was in wide-spread use by this tribe well into the mid-to-late 19th Century. John Ewers' Blackfoot informants referred to this one-piece soft-soled footwear as "*real moccasin*". The style "survived to the end of buffalo days as the typical hair lined, winter moccasin" (Ewers, 1945:39). Hardsole moccasins, a style the Blackfoot apparently learned from other tribes, came into use by the middle of the 1800s. In adornment, Blackfoot moccasins "are characterized by relatively small areas of decoration, confined largely or entirely to the front, or toe and instep area" (Ibid:38, 40). Designs were simple. They might be executed in quillwork or beadwork, depending upon the time frame and the maker's preference. Fully beaded uppers were not typical.

Leggings were originally constructed from leather, but later, trade wool in navy blue or scarlet became popular. Women's leggings were knee-high and snug fitting, with "a single vertical seam" (Ibid:44). When the legging was worn, this seam lay to "the outside of the leg" (Wissler, 1910:127). Any decoration was limited to the lower portion of the leggings, which was visible below the dress. Lanes of adornment were often "arranged to give a striped effect" (Ibid:127).

At the time of Maximilian's visit, Blackfoot women were belting their dresses with soft hide belts. During the mid-to-late 19th Century the Blackfoot developed a particular fondness for tacked belts. These were made of thick harness leather adorned by numerous rows of common brass tacks. Many tribes made use of the tacked belt as well as wide, tacked pennants, and this fashion was taken to its zenith by the Blackfoot, Sioux, Ute and Ft. Berthold people. Some Blackfoot belts were over eight inches wide and long enough to wrap twice around a young woman's body with some left over for a long drop. Many Blackfoot tacked belts sported well over a thousand tacks! If she had a tacked belt, the Blackfoot woman probably had a matching tacked knife sheath. She would have worn it on her belt, suspended by a cord so it hung down on her thigh (Ibid:128).

Before the availability of blankets or fabric shawls, Blackfoot women wore a bison robe as a wrap (see illustration on page iv). Sometimes these were decorated. In museum collections — and in Blackfoot memory — the most common decorated robe-type is the "marked" or real painted robe (Ewers, 1945:20). This painted or quilled pattern consisted of five or more equally spaced narrow parallel lanes running lengthwise, head-to-tail on the robe. The lanes were typically broken at intervals into rectangular segments of differing color (Ibid:20), as illustrated in the robe on page 50.

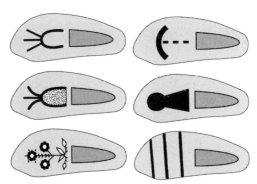

Figure 2.17 Typical Blackfoot moccasin designs as illustrated in *Blackfeet Crafts.*

Figure 2.18 Knife sheath using brass tacks for decoration. Illustration by Alex Koslov.

Figure 2.19 Heavily tacked belts were often worn by Blackfeet women. Illustration by Alex Koslov.

CROW STYLE: Tradecloth Dress

The Crow People have long been noted for elegant clothing with a distinctive style. In the 1830s, George Catlin wrote that the Crow "may be justly said to be the most beautifully clad of all the Indians in these regions." Crow women he said, were "decently dressed ... with great beauty and taste" (Catlin, 1973 Vol.1:192 & 51). Just what were these women wearing that would merit such a declaration?

The first substantial 19th century description of Crow womens' clothing is found in Antoine Larocque's 1805 journal. In it he describes dresses made of elk or mountain sheep skin, with cape-like sleeves that covered the wearer's arm from elbow to wrist, and a fringed hemline that hung just at or below mid-leg, as illustrated on page 2.

About thirty years later, Catlin painted a portrait of the Crow woman (0-je-en-a-he-ha "Woman Who Lives in a Bear's Den") wearing a two-hide dress. Rufus Sage, an early 1840's trapper, described Crow apparel in his book Rocky Mountain Life as having cape-like sleeves, lots of fringe, and decoration of metal tinklers, beads and porcupine quillwork. From primary references we can conclude that during the early 1800s Crow women were wearing classic Type 1 and Type 2 two-hide dresses (Lowie, 1922:226, and Mason 1926:398). The principal adornment on these dresses was quillwork or beadwork, typically laid out in long narrow strips (Lowie, 1920:302). [See Fig. 2.19, "Eva Sun Goes Slow"].

By the mid 1800s, Crow buckskin dresses were sporting the extensive elk tooth decoration that students of Plains Indian fashion tend to associate with the "reservation era". According to Rudolph F. Kurz, Crow women originated this form of ornamentation (Kurz, 1937:251). By the 1850s, some Crow dresses were "covered across the breast and back with rows of elk teeth and sea shells" (Denig, 1961:158). Museum examples of old Crow buckskin dresses with multiple rows of elk tooth ornamentation are rare. However, a sketch by Kurz (shown here) provide ample confirmation of their historic existence.

With the growing availability of yard goods during the mid-to-late 19th Century, Crow women began using wool tradecloth or saved-list cloth for their dresses. Tradecloth was a semi-coarse fabric in navy blue, scarlet or red, and occasionally kelly green. Although other tribes such as the Sioux and Blackfoot also developed tradecloth dress styles, Crow and other Plateau dresses have characteristics which set them apart. Among these characteristics are: true sleeves, long, narrow, and closed; a straight hemline with no side drops, and a yoke of contrasting color. If the dress is blue, the yoke — and perhaps also a band along the

wrist and hem — is red, and vice versa. The yoke piece is usually "outlined with a narrow lane of lazy stitch beadwork" (Holm, 1958:46). Crow tradecloth dresses were often lined with a "softer" fabric like muslin or calico, or were worn with a separate underdress.

Figure 2.20 Rudolph Kurz illustration, ca. 1851 that demonstrates the use of elk teeth as a form of decoration on women's dresses.

The elk tooth decoration of earlier hide dresses became the preferred decoration for the newer tradecloth ones. Dresses decorated with elk teeth became symbols of status in the Crow Nation. The number of elk teeth on his wife and daughter's dresses was "one of the indices of a man's wealth and importance" (Mason, 1926:398). Many of these dresses sported upward of 400 teeth. Since only the two "eye" teeth or incisors were used from any given bull elk, such a dress was positive proof of the hunting prowess and/or trading skills of the wearer's male relatives. A dress decorated with many rows of elk teeth also indicated the wearers rank and wealth (Schneider, 1968:15). According to Denig, who wrote about this in 1851, "the price of the elk teeth alone is 100 for a good horse or in money the value of $50" (Denig, 1961:158). Sometimes, due to the expense of genuine elk teeth, bone imitations were carved and substituted. This is a historic practice that continues today. Although real elk teeth are preferred, the use of imitations in no way lessens the respect due to the garment as a powerful symbol of Crow identity.

Trade cloth dresses have an elegance all their own. "They're not real easy [to make] and they're not real cheap [depending on the material you choose], but they're authentic and they can give you an outfit with as much beauty and style as anyone could desire" (Holm, 1958:43). According to Bill Holm, there were three general styles of tradecloth dresses: Northwestern, used by the Blackfoot and other Rocky Mountain tribes such as the Flathead and Nez Perce, Crow, used exclusively by this tribe, and Sioux, also used by the Northern Cheyenne and Arapaho. Historic photographs by Soule and others reveal yet another style worn by the Comanche, Kiowa and Kiowa-Apache. Because of notations in the journals of F. A. Larocque, we know for certain that the Crow people had access to wool tradecloth by at least 1805. In the summer of that year, Larocque used a fathom of scarlet saved-list cloth as partial payment for a horse he purchased from the Crow. That Upper Missouri people were wearing garments having red tradecloth with undyed selvage in their construction is evident through the journals of Prince Maximilian and the artwork of Karl Bodmer. By the middle of the

(continued on page 22)

"SAVED-LIST" TRADECLOTH

by Rex Reddick and Earl Fenner

Woolen cloth for the Indian trade, the bulk of which was originally produced in England, was of a distinct type made in several qualities. Known variously as "saved-list", "strouds", and "Indian cloths", it was primarily produced in either dark blue or scarlet, with a characteristic scalloped (sometimes called saw-tooth) edge, which was left in the white. This fabric was 100% wool, usually 54" in width, and highly desired by the Indians for use in clothing.

Saved-list cloth receives its name from its un-dyed or "saved" edges or "lists", the majority of which are approximately 1" to 1¼" wide. However, an 1838 shipping invoice to the American Fur Company lists 54 inch cloth in Indigo blue and scarlet with 1½" saved list. (AFC Papers, 1838). The cloth was woven from un-dyed, white wool yarn and then dyed "in the piece" to the desired color, with the "lists" or selvedges being saved from the dye. The Gloucestershire (Stroudwater basin) region of England had soft water, which was well suited to the piece dyeing process, and the cloth from this area was justly famous for its bright, solid colored cloths, especially scarlet, which was produced with dyes made from the cochineal beetle. (Mann, 1971:10-11). As this dye was quite expensive and because in tailoring the selvedges are normally cut off and discarded, a considerable savings could be realized by dyeing only that portion of the cloth intended for use.

The reasons for piece dyeing are simply explained and well documented. While it did not necessarily predominate over yarn dyeing during the period prior to the 20th century, the method was used primarily to obtain good, solid colors. First, it is almost impossible to keep red yarn from being contaminated by particles of white wool from the various other operations going on in the mill, and second, which is peculiar to the scarlet color produced from cochineal, is that it would not stand the subsequent operations, such as milling, fulling, etc. Further, the soaps used would dull or "sadden" the color of the scarlet. (Bemiss, 1815:208). Other cloth, such as "medleys", or mixed colors, were yarn dyed (dyed "in the wool"). (Mann, 1971:9-10, 46-47).

The finished cloth had natural, un-dyed selvedges approximately 1" to 1¼" in width, delineated by an irregular saw-tooth line (Conn, 1982:143). These were the result of heavy canvas bindings that had been sewn along the edges of the fabric, remaining in place throughout the dyeing process, and then being removed afterward. In fact, when looking at old strouding, it is not uncommon to see evidence of this binding: small holes and a semi-regular saw tooth pattern in the selvedge near the intersection of the dyed color and the white, un-dyed edge.

A thick cotton or linen binding, known as "girt-webbing", was hand sewn to the edges. It was folded in half, still being wide enough to cover the selvedge when it was then rolled up. After the selvedge had been rolled, the webbing was put around it so as to enclose it all, and was then sewn on with small twine, passing through the cloth close to the list, and drawn tightly over both, with the stitches being about one-fifth inch apart. After dyeing, the webbing and stitches were removed, thus leaving the white edges with the saw-tooth look. (Partridge, 1823:123).

According to James Clay & Sons, Ltd. in Halifax, England, the practice of protecting the edges from the dye was continued for the Indian trade in Canada until approximately 1956. (Cahoon, 1958). Even after less expensive aniline dyes were developed about 1850, and there was no longer a need to save the lists, these white edged wools remained so popular in the Indian trade that the practice was continued in order to meet the demand for purely decorative purposes.

Georg Barth (2003), through trial, error and experiments in dyeing cloth, has explained an unusual and interesting characteristic he has observed on most late 19th century examples of saved-list cloth as well as in photographs from that period. "You will notice a slight but distinctive curl along the edge; on the outer or convex side you will see there the familiar imprints of sewing, which have a slight curve. On the concave side (the 'inside'), however, you will see oblique and straight imprints. These clearly cannot result from the sewing as they usually do not align with the imprints of the sewing and must have been caused by a rope, around which the canvas-covered list was sewn. The imprints on old cloth are narrower and more delicate as more tightly twisted ropes may have been used. However, this characteristic is hardly ever found on earlier cloth from the Wied/Bodmer period (early 19th century).

This white edge, highly prized for its decorative quality, was of such importance to the Indian trade that John Mason, Superintendent of the Indian Office in Washington, D.C., stressed this in an 1811 letter to E. J. DuPont, inquiring as to his ability to manufacture cloth: "The colours, stripes &c must be particularly attended to for instance a cloth without a white stripe on the edge will not be worn by an Indian-or a Blanket without the points designated-if he can by any means procure such" (Peake, 1954:268).

In a subsequent letter to Messers. James Moore & Co. of Waterford, Virginia, Mason further defines the qualities of the cloth his office required:

"Strouds (a very coarse cloth) should be six quarters wide and weigh when dressed from 18 to 20 ounces per yard - to be coloured either dark blue or red principally the former - and to have a narrow stripe of white left in dying about an inch and one fourth from each edge as per samples - to be regularly put up in pieces of about 20 yards each.

"Indian Cloths should be six quarters wide and have a white stripe left in dying upon each side as per samples - coloured dark blue or red - quality about the same as samples" (Ibid:269).

Thus we see that there were different qualities of this white-edged cloth produced through the years. Further insight is gained from the prices quoted by Mason in his letter of 29 July 1812:

"The prices we have been accustomed to pay wholesale dealers for imported articles when foreign commerce was unrestricted were as follows—

for Strouds about $1 per yard,
for Red cloth which is generally of better quality than that dyed blue for same supply $1.75 to $2 per yard" (Ibid:).

Reference to the cloth is often found in historic texts as stroud cloth, strouds or strouding, although among modern scholars the generally accepted nomenclature is "saved-list" cloth. The term "stroud cloth" is obviously from the prominent wool-producing district around Stroud, England, which was especially well known for its brightly colored, scarlet cloth, and where this and other types of wool cloth were produced in great quantities. Several factors evidently contributed to the cloth from this region being so brightly colored. These include dyeing in the piece after the cloth was scoured and fulled, the skill of the dyers that developed over a long period of time, and the unique characteristics of the water in the Stroudwater basin. (Mann, 1971:10-11).

A very nice replica of saved-list cloth can be achieved with a good quality woolen material by sewing on a white binding that has been cut with pinking shears to give the appearance of a saw tooth edge. Further, this is an authentic technique that was often used in the past when genuine saved-list cloth was not available or unaffordable.

We would like to extend our sincere thanks to Georg Barth, Sam Cahoon, Allen Chronister, Pat Hartless, Rick Hewitt, Bill Holm, Bob Laidig, Benson Lanford, Joe Rivera and Bob Voelker for sharing their knowledge with us as well as their help in furnishing various samples of original saved-list cloth for study.

(continued from page 20)

1800's we begin encountering primary journal entries that refer specifically to Crow women wearing tradecloth dresses. Many of these references also mention the dresses being adorned with rows of elk teeth. The following construction section is devoted to the production of a basic Crow style tradecloth dress which would be appropriate for use at historical re-enactments and powwows. Because the dress is only a part of the whole outfit, the construction section is followed by a discussion of accessories suitable for accompanying the mid-19th Century Crow style garment.

CONSTRUCTION

Structurally, the Crow style tradecloth dress is quite similar to the Sioux style which is covered in more detail in a separate section of this book, with two exceptions: the Crow garment has no long triangular gusset in the side seams, and the sleeves of the Crow garment are true sleeves that taper to closed wrists. Classic Crow tradecloth dresses are characterized by the yoke-like, cloth panel overlaid around the neck opening as previously mentioned. In the evolutionary sense, this panel is probably a vestige of the folded over yoke on earlier hide dresses. It is retained in a stylized form that pays tribute to the original while updating the look to fit the new medium of tradecloth. Sometimes Crow dresses also have a small panel of contrasting-color tradecloth at the wrist and along the bottom hem. If the dress is made of blue tradecloth, such panels are typically red, or vice versa.

Crow women made use of red tradecloth for their garments far more often than their Sioux counterparts who favored blue almost exclusively. Historic Crow women occasionally sported dresses of green tradecloth as well, though this practice should not be considered common.

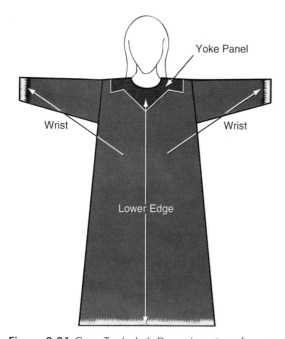

Figure 2.21 Crow Tradecloth Dress. Location of contrasting color areas.

MATERIALS

The materials listed below will be needed to construct a basic Crow style tradecloth dress with the typical, contrasting color yoke at the neck.

• Woolen tradecloth fabric: The most desirable fabric for a dress of this period is known as saved-list cloth, due to its characteristic white, saw-tooth edge. A more moderately priced substitute, and the next best choice, is good quality woolen material or trade wool with a plain edge. Popular colors were blue and occasionally red or green.

Figure 2.22 Photo of Sarah Grandmothers, wife of Harry Beads, Crow, Montana, ca. 1903-1910. Although from a later time period, this is still an excellent example of a typical Crow elk tooth dress, panel belt with brass tacks, moccasins and fully beaded leggings. Courtesy of Written Heritage, Photo No. 22034.

A beginner who is nervous about making those first few cuts into a pricey piece of top-of-the-line wool tradecloth will benefit cost-wise by experimenting with an inexpensive muslin the first time they undertake a tradecloth dress project. This allows some much-needed practice without sacrificing a costlier material. Muslin is an excellent choice, as the resulting mock up is very practical and will help ensure proper fit and proportions. It can then become the underdress, which is washable. This technique works equally well for fitting moccasins, too.

The ideal fabric width is 54" to 60" wide and the color should be either a very dark indigo or navy blue, kelly green, or a bright scarlet which was a deep, true red. Historically, the dye used to obtain this rich scarlet hue was produced from the cochineal beetle. Today, wool tradecloth is available in a wide array of colors including purple and yellow; however, if you wish to achieve a middle 1800's look to your outfit, I suggest avoiding these newer colors and sticking to blue or red.

If the intended wearer is a medium-framed woman, construction of the garment will require at least three yards of 60" wide wool tradecloth or broadcloth, plus one yard of a contrasting color. If you wish to be on the safe side and/or think you might want to make matching tradecloth leggings, purchasing four or five yards of your primary color tradecloth is optimal.

Remember that this project is based on the specific measurements of the intended wearer. Other dress sizes will require more or less fabric, so purchase with this in mind.

Special note: Crow tradecloth dresses are always worn either with a cloth "underdress" (see figure 2.25) or are lined with cotton/muslin cloth, so you must choose one of these options. Lining at least the upper part of the dress, the area where the elk teeth are attached, is advisable to support the cloth and does not obviate the need for an underdress. If you decide to make a separate underdress (which is quite practical because you can also wear it by itself if you choose), you can use the same directions for the basic tradecloth dress, minus any contrasting panels. Just shorten the hem by an inch or two so that when the two dresses are worn together, the underdress isn't readily visible peeking from under the tradecloth one. Purchase the same amount of fabric. Or you can opt to simply line the tradecloth dress by pinning a softer cloth to the wool fabric then cutting and sewing as per the directions, being careful to

Figure 2.23
Wool tradecloth with the characteristic rainbow selvedge edge in multi-colored stripes. Photo courtesy of Crazy Crow Trading Post.

Figure 2.24
Saved-list cloth, the earliest type tradecloth, showing the characteristic white saw-tooth edge. Photo courtesy of Crazy Crow Trading Post.

Figure 2.25 This Crow woman wears a fine saved-list cloth dress adorned with a number of elk teeth. Instead of a hide robe, she is wrapped in what appears to be a trade blanket with a bound edge. Note the underdress protruding from her sleeves. Courtesy of Written Heritage, Photo No. 35219.

19th Century Plains Indian Dresses

work so that the lining is always on the inside of the garment. Regardless of the option you choose, the alternate fabric could be a two-color cotton calico or linen fustian, a plain color cotton broadcloth (no exotic colors, please!), or perhaps even ticking in the classic red-white or blue-white stripe pattern.

- **Thread:** Cotton or linen; a spool the same color as both of your tradecloth fabric choices. If you are making an underdress, purchase a spool of thread to match this as well.
- **Bias Tape/Ribbon: white, dark blue or red:** For finishing the neck opening, plus cuffs and hem if desired.
- **Scissors:** dressmaker quality
- **Tape Measure & Yard Stick**
- **Pins:** Straight dressmaker's pins + medium-size safety pins
- **Needles:** An all-purpose sharp, plus a narrow tapestry needle with a long eye.
- **Seamstress' Chalk:** For marking off dimensions on fabric, etc.
- **Sewing Machine:** The basic Crow style tradecloth garment and the cotton cloth underdress can be sewn by machine if desired. Or they can be successfully sewn by hand by the careful and confident seamstress. This is largely a matter of personal preference, dictated by the intended use of the completed garment, as well as time, skill and other factors.

DECORATION

The traditional adornment for the Crow style tradecloth dress is elk teeth. Whether you use genuine elk teeth or manufactured imitations is again determined by factors such as availability, personal preference, and your pocket book. Genuine elk teeth are costly. This has led to the marketing of a variety of realistic looking imitations, most of which have pre-drilled holes which save time and effort. Crow women typically attached elk teeth to their tradecloth dresses with white cotton cord or thin, light colored leather thongs. Simulated sinew is also an excellent modern substitute as it is quite strong.

MEASUREMENTS

The following wearer's measurements, in inches, must be taken using the tape measure:

1. Hip. Measure all the way around, then divide in half, and add 2 inches.
2. Hip #2. Measure all the way around, then divide in half, and add 10 inches.
3. Top of shoulder to lower calf. Note that most all old dresses fall well below the knee.
4. Measure from point of shoulder to wrist to determine sleeve length.
5. Point of shoulder to 3 inches beneath arm pit.
6. Circumference of wrist, plus 2 inches.

FABRIC LAYOUT

Spread the fabric out on a large surface so it lays flat. Orient the fabric horizontally, with the selvedge at top and bottom as in Figure 2.27. Use the measurements you recorded to mark these fabric dimensions:

1. A to B and C to D. Both of these distances are Measurement #2 (hip divided in half plus ten inches). This is the bottom edge of the dress body. Note that you are making two identical measurements because you are creating the front and the back of the dress (Piece 1 and Piece 2). Use two safety pins to superimpose Measurement #1 (hip divided in half plus two inches) centered, on lines A-B and C-D. Then use safety pins to mark the ends of Measurement #1 on both. These are points a, b and c, d.

2. Using the safety pins as reference, measure upward toward the top of the fabric the distance of measurement #3 (top of shoulder to lower calf). Transfer the safety pins to both points on each body piece. These are points E, F and G, H. These points (E, F and G, H) should be exactly the distance apart of Measurement #1 (hip divided in half plus two inches).

3. From points E, F and G, H, measure downward (toward the bottom edge of the fabric) the distance of

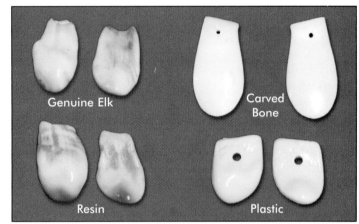

Figure 2.26 Various types of "elk teeth": genuine, and carved bone on top row; plastic and resin, below.

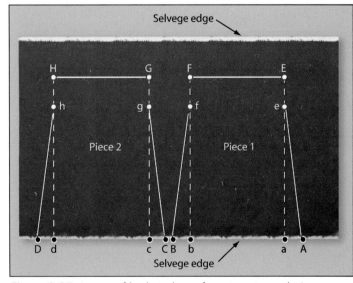

Figure 2.27 Layout of body is shown for orientation only. Lay out should maximize the use of the material here and in Fig. 2.28 as well.

Measurement #5 (point of shoulder to 1 ½ inches beneath arm pit). Mark these points securely. They are shown as e, f and g, h on Figure 2.27.

4. Draw a line between points E & F and points G & H. Draw lines between points A & e, B & f, C & g, and D & h. Cut out both body piece so formed. These are Pieces 1 & 2.

If you are using plain wool cloth with no selvedge, you can now sew bias tape, ribbon, or cloth binding on all the edges marked as selvedge on Figure 2.27 & 2.28. Sew carefully. At the corners the binding should be folded neatly and sewn tightly closed. Crease the binding with an iron, if necessary. A binding of contrasting color serves the same visual purpose as the white selvage. It adds a touch of color contrast to the dress as well as helping to prevent fraying and stress-related rips.

To prevent fraying and tearing during wear., it is recommended that you take the time to "bind" all cut edges of the wool cloth pieces using a zigzag stitch on a sewing machine. For added security, you can also turn under this edge a quarter inch and use a running stitch to tack it down.

SLEEVES

This sleeve work is shown in Figure 2.28. Use measurement #6 to mark off lines I-J and K-L. Leave plenty of room between them to allow for the tapering required. Mark the exact center of line I-J and K-L as points x and x1. From points x and x1, use seamstress' chalk to draw a vertical line point upward the length of measurement #4 plus 1 ½ inches. Mark these two new points (y and y1) with pins. Measure outward horizontally left and right from points y and y1 the distance of measurement #5. Mark these four distances off as points M, N, O, and P. The distance from point M to point N and point O to point P are equal and are measurement #5 doubled.

Extend lines x-y and x1-y1 upward another one-and-a-half inches to determine new points z & z1. Mark these with safety pins. Draw a curving line to connect points M-z-N and poinis O-z1-P. These lines now form the outline of Pieces 3 and 4, the

sleeves. Cut them out. Use bias tape or contrasting color cloth to bind Edges I-J and K-L of the sleeves. If you are lining your trade-cloth, careful catch both layers of fabric within the binding! With the fabric wrong side out, sew both sleeves closed from wrist point I/J to shoulder point M/N and Wrist Point K/L to Shoulder Point O/P. Keep the finished sleeves wrong side out for now.

THE NECK OPENING

Lay Pieces 1 & 2 on top of each other with right sides of the fabric facing inward toward each other. Pin them together across the top, a few inches from the edge. Find the exact center of the top edge. From there, measure outward 3 ½ inches to the right and the left, and mark these points as Q and R. Connect these two points with a rounded scooping u-shaped line (see Figure 2.29). This is the oval of the neck opening of the dress. Cut it out carefully. Leaving a quarter inch seam allowance, sew across F/G-Q and E/H-R. These are the shoulder seams. Remove pins holding Pieces 1 & 2 together.

Use bias tape or cotton cloth to bind the hemed edges of both Pieces 1 & 2, all the way across. Ribbon is rarely seen on Crow dresses. Hand sewing is recommended with small tight stitches. When the hem binding is complete, lay out the unfinished garment right side up a shown in Figure 2.29.

YOKE PANEL

Using the measurements shown in Figure 2.30, mark off and cut out this yoke panel from the single yard of contrasting-color tradecloth. Pin the panel securely in place atop the shoulder/neck opening area as completed in the previous section. This will

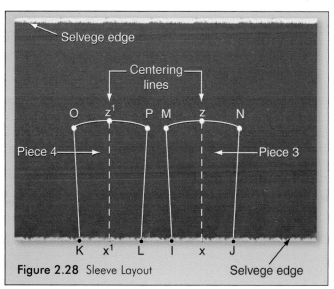

Figure 2.28 Sleeve Layout

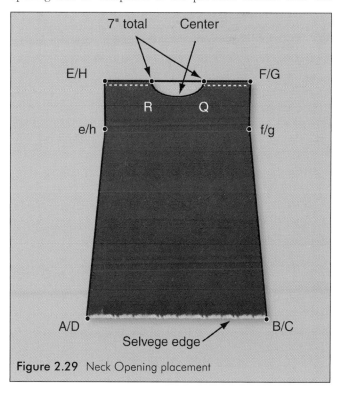

Figure 2.29 Neck Opening placement

19th Century Plains Indian Dresses

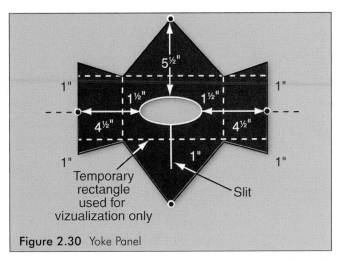

Figure 2.30 Yoke Panel

require quite a number of pins. Be sure the oval of the neck opening is identical in shape. Again, the yoke panel must be pinned to the dress securely. For the wearer to get her head in and out of the neck opening will require the making of a small access slit (see Figure 2.30). You must make this slit now. Using a pair of scissors, cut a four inch long slit downward from the middle of the neck opening. Do this on one side only, the side which is to be the back of the finished garment.

Use bias tape or cotton cloth to bind the entire neck opening. It is recommended that you do this binding by hand sewing, using small tight stitches. You will be catching two layers of fabric within this binding (unless you are also sewing a lining into the garment, which means you will be catching three layers of fabric -lining, dress, yoke panel -within the binding!). Begin sewing/binding at the bottom of the slit. Work up and around the neck opening oval, then back down the other slide of the slit. Be especially careful with your stitches so that the binding lies flat. Secure the bottom of the slit with a few extra stitches to prevent tearing. Sew the yoke panel to the dress itself by using a wide zigzag stitch. After this is done, remove all pins.

Now is the time to outline the yoke panel (effectively covering the zigzag stitching) with a single lane of lane stitch beadwork. Historically, white seed beads were commonly used and the lane is narrow, from six to eight beads wide, or approximately $3/8$" to $5/16$", as would be used on moccasins. The outlining of the yoke panel with a lane of lane stitch beadwork visually helps set apart the panel from the rest of the dress, giving it a pleasing contrast that becomes especially important when the elk tooth adornment is added.

Note: If you plan to add elk teeth to the dress, these can be attached before the sides and sleeves of the dress are sewn together, as it is much easier to lay out the teeth identically on both sides of the dress and to lace them on. Another method is to hang the finished dress on a mannequin or dressform and lay out the adornment in this way, so as to obtain a true feel for the visual, three-dimensional quality. See "Decoration" section.

SIDES

With the dress inside out sew the two side seams (B/C to f/g, and A/D to e/h). Leave a quarter inch seam allowance. Leave the garment inside out. See Figure 2.29.

SLEEVES

From the inside of the insideout garment, fit finished sleeve Piece 3 in to one arm hole. You will be pinning it in place, beginning at the shoulder point. Ease the sleeve into the opening as you proceed downward going from side-to-side as needed to fit the sleeve into place. Points M/N of sleeve Piece 3 will eventually meet point f/g squarely. After the sleeve is pinned in position, sew it securely into place. Leave a quarter inch seam allowance. Repeat this process with sleeve Piece 4, beginning at the shoulder point and eventually lining up Point O/P on Piece 4 with point e/h. See Figure 2.31.

After sewing both sleeves in place, turn the garment right side out. Attach two tie thongs, one on each side of the top of the neck slit. These enable the neck opening to be tied closed in back after the wearer has inserted her head through it.

DECORATION

It is recommended that you lay the dress out on a flat surface before sewing it together, and then experiment with placement of the elk teeth by laying them on the dress as you want them to lie when the garment is finished. Move them around to determine the best arrangement and overall look. Carry the pattern right out onto the sleeves, too, remembering to keep the distance between the rows equal. This aids in the overall aesthetic quality of the pattern. See Figure 2.32.

To help you determine how many elk teeth you will need for your project, first make a careful study of original Crow tradecloth dresses, either by going to view museum collections, or by looking through a number of collection catalogs. Note the number of rows of elk teeth, and how many teeth are in each row. Then ask yourself how many rows of teeth you desire for your garment. On dresses from the late 19th century, it is not unusual to count over four hundred elk teeth, invariably of the carved bone type, on one side of historic Crow dresses. This means that

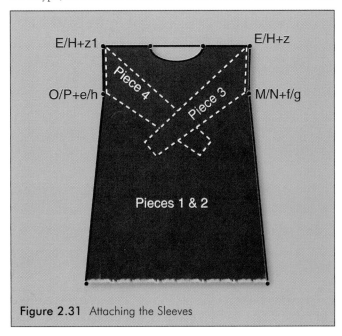

Figure 2.31 Attaching the Sleeves

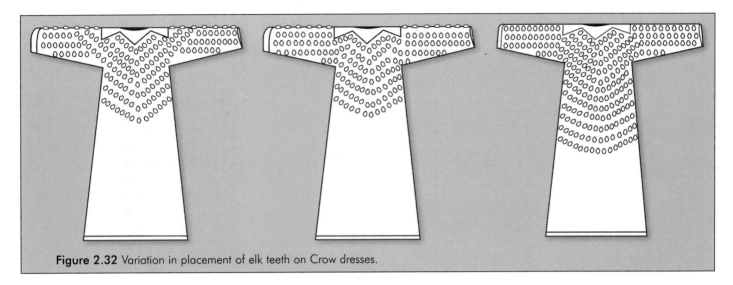

Figure 2.32 Variation in placement of elk teeth on Crow dresses.

there are actually over eight hundred teeth on such a garment because the front and the back are identically adorned, although this is not always visible in photographs.

More important than the number of teeth used, however, is the appropriate amount of spacing between the individual teeth as well as between the rows. One of the most prevalent mistakes seen on modern dresses is improper spacing — either too few or too many teeth that are either too far apart or too close together. The proper situation of teeth is crucial for the appropriate look.

It is also mandatory to point the teeth in the correct directions, particularly on the sleeves. On the yoke proper, the rows are arranged in shallow arcs, and the teeth toward the outer ends of each row point slightly outward. Study the photos and the detailed illustrations for these points.

Be sure to record the arrangement you have chosen so that you can duplicate it on the other side of the dress as well. Write or sketch it out, or take a Polaroid snapshot, etc. If the teeth are laid out before the sides are sewn up, recording of the arrangement will not be necessary since the front and back will be done at the same time.

There are several methods of marking the dress for the the location of each tooth. A tiny dot of white fabric marker works well, but you must decide exactly how the dots should be placed in relationship to the teeth themselves so as to assure uniform placement.

Modern Crows have hit upon a very clever and workable method. They lay out the teeth and adjust them until they are in perfect arrangement. Then they put a dot of glue (such as "Duco Cement") on the back of each tooth, one at a time and set the

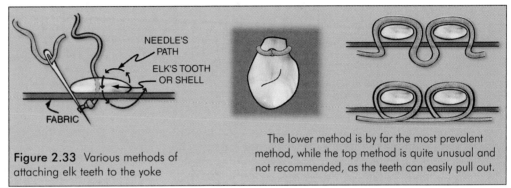

Figure 2.33 Various methods of attaching elk teeth to the yoke

The lower method is by far the most prevalent method, while the top method is quite unusual and not recommended, as the teeth can easily pull out.

tooth back in place, letting the glue dry before lacing the teeth to the fabric. This ensures exactness of placement, but also helps to keep the teeth from subsequently slipping from under the lacings, which can be a real problem. If this method offends the purists, remember that Indians have always been innovators who are extremely adept at perfecting their own material culture. If you prefer not to use glue, then the dot method is best.

Use the cord and a tapestry needle to sew on the elk teeth in horizontal or gently sloping, yet horizontal, rows. Remember to use three points of attachment for each tooth, as shown in Figure 2.33. This optimizes the security of the attachment, while minimizing the potential for the teeth to slip around and/or stick out (which can be quite embarrassing if one or two of them stick out in the wrong places). I also recommend that you do not do more than three or four tooth attachments without looping back through the fabric and securing the cord with a small knot on the inside of the garment. In fact, for optimal peace of mind, it is best to secure each tooth independently of the others! Yes, this requires a lot of knotting and threading, but it's worth it to not have to worry about losing a whole row or section of a row of teeth to an unforeseen knot slippage or cord break.

Figure 2.34 Classic Crow dress of dark blue wool decorated with both genuine elk teeth augmented with carved bone teeth. The number of teeth probably indicated the husband's hunting prowess and acted as charms of longevity. Note the characteristic, triangular neck panel of contrasting color wool. Private collection. Photo by Jessica Reddick.

Figure 2.35 Crow Type-2, two-hide dress, adorned with large polychrome beads, tradecloth pieces, and an overall coating of red pigment. Though collection data places this dress ca. 1870, its construction and decoration are comfortably within mid-19th. century parameters. Chicago Field Museum display. Courtesy of Written Heritage Collection. Photo by Joe Kazumura.

CROW STYLE Accessories

In order to achieve an optimum mid-l9th Century "look", one must choose suitable accessories to complement the Crow style tradecloth dress. Typical female dress codes of the day seem to point to four requisite items: leggings, moccasins, belt and robe or plaid type shawl. Let's look at these in a bit more detail and, where possible, note any specifically Crow characteristics which will be helpful in recreating them.

Crow women's leggings from the early-to-middle-1800's were snug-fitting unfringed tubes made of lightweight deer or antelope skin or occasionally, of wool tradecloth. They were held up by a leather garter tied at the knee (Sage, 1982:89). Worn oriented to the front, the single seam of these leggings might be covered or "hidden" with a lane or two of blue beads worked in the lane stitch, or a row of early trade type small brass buttons (Larocque, 1910:177). Leggings of tradecloth were often beaded in a distinctive series of horizontally-oriented lane-stitch lanes. These lanes were usually all one color, typically in light blue or white. From what we can gather from primary sources, it seems that at this point in time, Crow women were not sewing leggings and moccasins together into a "boot" form.

The oldest Crow moccasin type is the side-seam (Lessard, 1980:66), therefore it is this type which best serves the mid-19th Century impression. Moccasins may be left plain, or decorated with a bit of beadwork or quillwork. U-shaped and "keyhole"-shaped designs (see Figure 2.37) centered on the moccasin upper, were two of the most common adornment motifs on historic Crow women's moccasins (Lowie, 1922:226). Sometimes the U shape was accompanied by other design elements, including "feathers and bars".

Crow women always belted their dresses. Earlier soft hide belts were gradually replaced by highly stylized panel belts made of heavy harness leather. Crow panel belts characteristically had "three beaded sections separated by segments of plain leather. The beaded panels were of long, loose, lane-stitch bead rows, edged by single vertical rows of overlay beading. "When the belt was worn, the beadwork tightened up" (Koch, 1977:85). This type belt should be beaded with the ends secured so that the belt forms an oval similar to the way it will in wear. In this manner the long, lengthwise "lane stitches" of beads are of the proper length -- they therefore sag when the belt is layed out flat. The unbeaded portions of

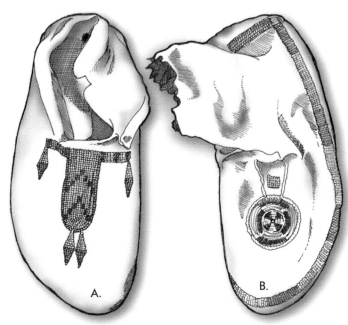

Figure 2.37. Examples of Crow Moccasins from the American Museum of Natural History.

A. "U" figure with "feathers".

B. Circle or "Club Head" style, sometime referred to as a "keyhole" design.

Figure 2.36 Antique Shawls of the type favored by Plains Indian women. Left: Plaid wool with cotton warp. Right: Floral embroidery on wool, collected at Rosebud Sioux Reservation. Courtesy Benson Lanford Collection. Photo by Benson Lanford.

Crow panel belts were sometimes adorned with simple tackwork using small brass tacks. Silver colored tacks, however, were also used. In examining historic photographs, it seems they were almost always worn with the fastener/buckle in front.

Matching "belt sets" consisitng of awl case, strike-a-light pouch and small possible pouch are not representative of the historic Crow wardrobe. Instead, the Crow woman might sport a knife in a sheath which matched her belt, and carry a roughly square bag made from the tanned skin of the lower portion of several elk legs, including the dew claws, or a small soft hide pouch with an oversized, fully-beaded closure flap which hung lower than the bottom edge of the pouch itself. This flap was often edged by a narrow lane of lane stitch beadwork.

Each Crow woman had a bison or elk hide robe, or plaid shawl or trade blanket to complete her ensemble. One manner of robe adornment which was quite popular among Crow women was that of multiple stripes, oriented horizontally within a roughly rectangular area. In the early 1800's this design would have been executed in painting or quillwork. By the mid 1800's it was being executed in lane stitch beadwork. The lanes were widely spaced, and though oriented horizontally, bore internal elaboration that gave the overall pattern a vertical feel. Beaded robes of this type were generally made of elk and were often included in the goods exchanged between two Crow families being united through marriage (Merritt, 1988:41).

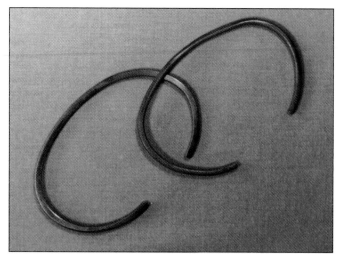

Figure 2.39 Antique Bracelets, very simply made by forming brass wire. Courtesy of Benson Lanford Collection. Photo by Benson Lanford.

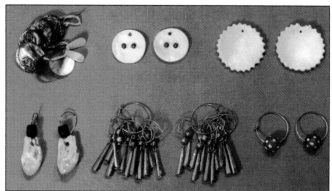

Figure 2.40 **Top row are Nez Perce, antique earrings:** 4 pairs of shell earings on a thong, a pair shell earrings with brass spots, and a pair of shell earrings with serrated margins. **Bottom row are replicas:** Pair of elk teeth with faceted cobalt beads, a pair of clustered ball-and-cone earrings, and a pair of wire loops with white-spotted beads. Courtesy of Benson Lanford Collection. Photo by Benson Lanford.

Figure 2.38. Necklace of antique, white-lined red beads (replica). Note detail of the method of cowrie shell attachment. Courtesy of Benson Lanford Collection. Photo by Benson Lanford.

Figure 2.41 **Necklaces (from left). Sioux:** antique hairpipes and hollow brass beads. **Ute:** antique, mixed wound beads, including many Chinese beads. **Modern Brass Beads** (small, replica). **Antique White-Lined-Red Beads** (replica). **"Pony Trader Blue"** antique wound beads (replica). Courtesy of Benson Lanford Collection. Photo by Benson Lanford.

Chapter 3:
CENTRAL PLAINS

The central Great Plains stretches roughly from the "middle" Missouri River southward to the Arkansas River. Although predominately a region of gently rolling grassland, this region also includes the mountainous Black Hills, and the Wichita Mountains in Oklahoma.

Sioux Woman's Dress, ca. 1850
This early, classic, two-skin dress was for ceremonies and other special occasions.
Native tanned hide, wool cloth, glass beads, sinew sewn. Length, 140 cm.
Private collection.

SIOUX STYLE: Sidefold Dress

ribes such as the Sioux, Pawnee and Arapaho (whose historical economy was largely horse-and-bison based) inhabited the Central Plains. Certain segments of other tribes — most notably the "Wind River" Shoshone, but also the eastern bands of the Ute and Nez Perce and the Apache, exhibited many of the cultural characteristics anthropologists associate with the more "classic" historic Plains peoples, including mode of dress. Hence, along with a detailed look at three Sioux dress types, this chapter also looks briefly at Shoshone, Nez Perce and Ute garments.

A significant number of historical figures who were connected with the fur trade in the Rocky Mountain west during the first half of the 19th Century associated and/or allied themselves with these tribes by marriage. Because of these tribes' position as "middle men" in tribal trade routes, such an arrangement was mutually profitable. Tribal members were assured a reliable supply of Euro-American goods, and traders benefited by the wide-reaching commerce of their customers.

A strong argument can be raised that because of their position as social middle-men, the material culture of tribes such as the Shoshone and Ute was extremely fluid and adaptive, particularly when it came to elements of clothing style and adornment. A great deal of innovative borrowing took place between these tribes and those with whom they had regular commerce, including the Teton, Cheyenne, Crow and Arapaho. In fact, enough of this borrowing took place to cause speculation as to who really influenced whom and to what extent. In our exploration of women's clothing we will encounter this fluidity of fashion.

Although there is some scholarly debate over the exact position of the sidefold dress in the developmental evolution of Plains Indian women's clothing, the sidefold is clearly an old style, and most probably an ancient one at that. It was in use for several decades before and after 1800. The writings of noted American Indian art authority Norman Feder contain the most significant compilations and assessments of information about this particular garment type. Feder has made a careful study of all of the sidefold dresses known to exist in museum collections. He groups them loosely into two types: Cree and Sioux, delineated primarily by structure and adornment characteristics (Feder, 1984:48-55, 75, 77).

Unlike the Cree-type sidefold dresses made from one large folded hide, the Sioux-type dresses located for study were made from two separate pieces of skin. These had been sewn together horizontally and the wide, folded-down top flap effectively covered this horizontal midriff seam. The flap might be adorned with painted designs. A narrow flounce, decorated with pony beadwork, was often sewn on along the hemline (Paterek, 1994:135). Quilled stripes, oriented horizontally, typically ornament the bottom half of Sioux-type sidefold dresses.

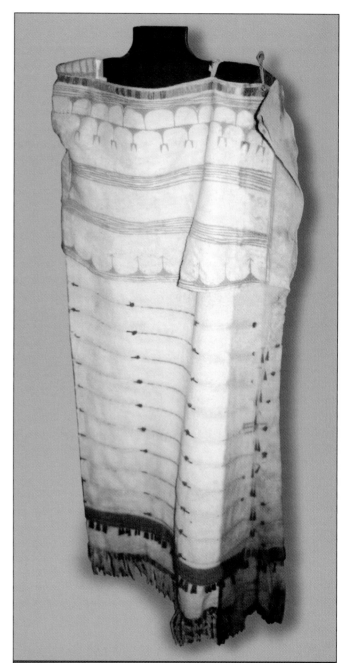

Figure 3.1 The simplicity of this early Sioux woman's dress, dating from approximately 1830, adds to its aesthetic charm. The cape-like upper part of the garment, to which the longer skirt has been sewn, is supported by means of a leather strap over the right shoulder and leather thongs which tie over the left shoulder. These thongs are somewhat of an unusual variation and the skirt does not actually "protrude" as it seems in the photo. Musee de l'Homme, Paris. Catalog No. 09.19.60. Photo by Ginger Reddick.

Rosemary Lessard comments, "If one folded down the top quarter of a quilled [bison] robe, wrapped it around the wearer and sewed up the open side, the process would produce a garment closely resembling the sideseam dress." Hence, she links the evolution of the sidefold style with the use of the classically-decorated bison robe, "which was a common covering for all Lakota women in the bison-hunting days" (Lessard, 1980:71).

CONSTRUCTION

To re-create the historic sidefold dress you must begin with optimal materials. If you are a small framed woman, a single very large elk hide might be adequate to produce your garment. To be sure, do a "test measure" of the hide. Here's how: while keeping the hide butt-end up, wrap the hide all the way around you, you should have enough leather to go completely around your body comfortably, if the edges were joined by a straight vertical seam. At the same time, fold the top of the hide down horizontally to form a 10-12" wide flap. Check this measurement carefully, as it might need to be proportionately wider depending on the size of the wearer. Hold the fold to the top of your shoulder. The head end of the hide must still hang down to your mid-to-upper calf. If you cannot do this with a single hide, and most people cannot, you will need to purchase two large deer hides and sew them together horizontally as in Figure 3.2. Be sure to keep the same ends of the hides facing the same direction. Use a yard stick to draw a straight line all the way across one edge of each hide. Cut off this excess

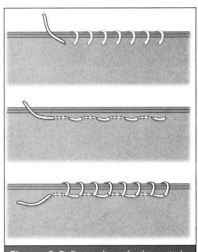

strip. Sew the two hides together as shown. Use a combination of a very tight running stitch with a whip stitch. Leave no more than a ¼" seam allowance and keep your stitches very small as in Figure 3.3.

The structure of the sidefold dress is based on folds. When using brain-tan leather the texture is similar on both sides of the hides; however, the hair side on most garments normally faced out. If you use commercially-tanned hides

Figure 3.3 Examples of whip stitch, running stitch and combination running/whip stitch.

and want to keep the texture of the dress body and yoke flap the same (which is strongly recommended), you must use two hides. When sewn together horizontally, the "top" hide must have the slick side facing up and the bottom hide must have the rough side facing up. You must also plan ahead carefully so that fold A-B allows enough leather for the flap, which hangs down over (and covers) the horizontal seam. This keeps the slick texture and the horizontal seam hidden neatly underneath the flap itself.

Because most readers will be utilizing the method of two-hides joined-horizontally, we will proceed with the construction in this manner. If you are using a single hide, the basic directions remain the same... just remember to keep your hide oriented with the butt-end up.

MATERIALS
- **Straight Pins** - heavy duty.
- **Needle & Sewing Awl**- you can use a sewing awl to pierce holes for your seams, or if you prefer, you can use a medium size Glover's needle to sew with, rather than piercing holes with the awl.
- **Seamstress Chalk** - or other marking device.
- **Tape Measure** - Yard Stick, 12 " Ruler.
- **Scissors** - good sharp shears that will cut easily through the thick elk leather. Many prefer to cut leather using a knife against a wooden board, a traditional method.
- **Thread Medium** - I recommend artificial sinew, split down to ¼ thickness.
- **Work Surface** - a large flat well-lit area.

You will need to take two (2) measurements to complete the sidefold dress, being careful not to make it fit too snugly. If the dress is too tight, it not only looks bad, but the wearer cannot move properly, much less sit or bend over.

1. Around the widest part of your hips (add 6" and divide this number in half).
2. Around over your shoulder, from the top to your armpit and back (add 6" and divide this number in half).

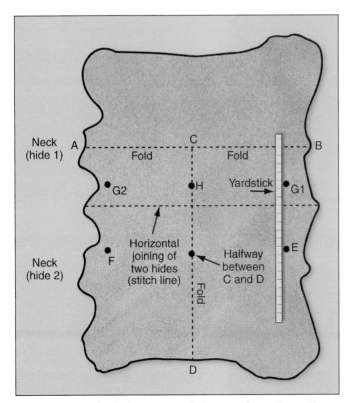

Figure 3.2 Method of joining two hides in order to "create" one large hide.

LAYING OUT THE DRESS BODY

Lay the leather as shown in Figure 3.3. With straight pins, lay out and carefully mark Fold Lines A-B and C-D. Fold Line A-B should be marked (with pins) on the back side of the hide as well as the front. This becomes very important later. Mark the point midway between C and D. Using the figure from your hip measurement (hip+2", divided by 2) measure outward from this middle point horizontally to the left and to the right. Mark these two points as E and F in Figure 3.2.

Using the yardstick vertically as shown in Figure 3.3, mark off your shoulder measurement (shoulder circumference +2", divided by 2) downward from Fold Line A-B in three places: directly above Point E, on Fold Line C-D, and directly above Point F. These are shown as Points G1, G2, and H on Figure 3.4. You may draw a vertical line from Fold A-B through Point G1 to E, continuing it downward and then tapering gently out toward the bottom and the top, as shown in Figure 3.4. Cut along this line avoiding any straight pins, and remove the strip of leather. Do the same thing to the left side, drawing a vertical line from fold A-B through Point G2 to F with tapering ends as shown. If needed, the left side of the hide may be temporarily folded back under the right so you can use the section you have already cut out and removed as a tracing guide.

Next, draw a horizontal line across the lower end of the leather. Taper the ends downward as shown in Figure 3.4. Cut along this line and remove the strip of leather. Fold the hide along Fold C-D, turning the left side of the hide up and over, until the sides meet so the rough side of the bottom hide is "in" toward itself (See Figure 3.5) Line up Points G1 and G2. Start sewing there. Using a combination running/whip stitch, continue sewing toward the bottom of the garment until you reach the point where the line begins to taper outward. This is the side seam of the dress; it will eventually be worn down your left side. Tie off the thread securely. You now have a roughly tube-shaped structure, with a line of pins marking Fold A-B. Leave the garment inside out.

COMPLETING SHOULDER AND NECK AREA

Continue construction of the dress after you have turned it right side out. Lay out the dress as in Figure 3.5. If you are using commercially-tanned leather the slick side is now "out" (visible) on the upper portion of the dress. This construction section is dependent on your having marked Fold A-B with straight pins on both sides of your leather (see Step One). With a few straight pins, mark off a neck opening in the middle of Fold A-B (as in Figure 3.6). Mark this opening on both the front and back of the dress but *do not cut this opening!* The neck opening, though imaginary, must be realistic in dimension. The only purpose for marking off this opening is so you can tell how long the seam will be that lies on your right shoulder.

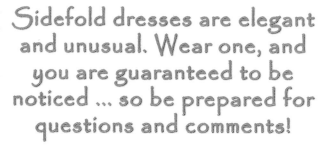

Sidefold dresses are elegant and unusual. Wear one, and you are guaranteed to be noticed ... so be prepared for questions and comments!

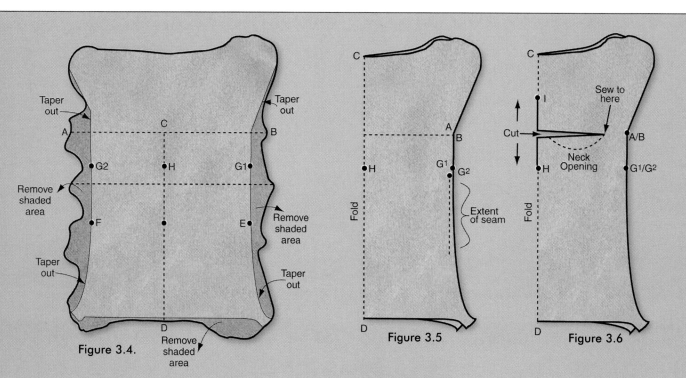

Figure 3.4.

Figure 3.5.

Figure 3.6.

You will now be connecting the front of the dress to the back of the dress, along the shoulder seam. Beginning at Point A/B and using a combination stitch again, sew along Fold A-B to the edge of the "neck opening". Take a few extra reinforcing stitches and tie off your thread securely. It is important to do this well, because this particular stitch point takes a lot of stress. Before you proceed you need to measure the length of this seam for future reference. Now remove all of the straight pins from the inside and outside of your garment tube. From this point on, you should use the pin holes as visual guides to your fold lines.

Mark Point I, as shown on Figure 3.6. Point I is the same distance above Fold A-B as Point H is below it. With your scissors, cut along Fold A-B, ending within ½" of your horizontal shoulder seam. Insert the scissors along Fold C-D. Cut upward to point I, and downward to Point H (see Figure 34). Fold the top of the hide downward along Fold A-B and the short horizontal shoulder seam. A flap will be formed to the front and back. The layout of the garment should be similar to that shown in Figure 3.8.

FINISHING THE SHOULDER

The opening in the dress for your right arm has sliced through two layers of leather in both the front and back. Beginning at Points U and U', sew these two layers together using a very small whip stitch around the outside edge, as in Figure 3.9. Do this for about six inches. Keep your stitches small, tight, and uniform.

The sidefold dress is held up on the right shoulder by a "strap". This is a separate piece of leather (use a scrap) that must be sewn onto the dress. The strap should be a little over half the length of the horizontal shoulder seam you have already sewn. It should be about 2" wide at one end, tapering to one inch at the other (see Figure 3.10). Use Figure 3.11 as a guide for positioning the strap. Remember when you sew it in place that you will be sewing through three layers of leather (strap/flap/body). You must also be careful to keep the correct rough texture of the strap showing. Sew the strap to the back side of the dress first, and do it so the seam itself will be toward the inside of the dress when it is worn. Use the combination stitch again. When this is complete, sew the strap to the front side of the dress, again sewing so the seam will be on the inside. The finished shoulder arrangement is shown in Figure 3.12.

Your completed sidefold dress should be worn with the vertical Fold C-D in Figures 3.5 to 3.6 oriented down your right side. You are wearing the garment correctly if the small strap is over your right shoulder, and the tabs of leather on the yoke and hemline are hanging to your left. The "short sleeves" of the sidefold dress make it an excellent garmet for warm summer weather, and for occasions where working in a sleeved dress might be awkward. Sidefold dresses are elegant and unusual. Wear one, and you are guaranteed to be noticed ... so be prepared for questions and comments.

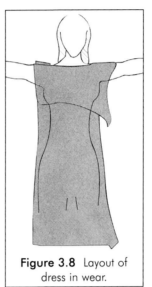

Figure 3.8 Layout of dress in wear.

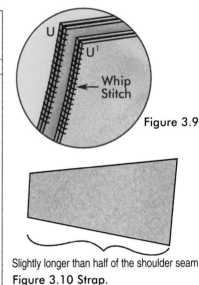

Figure 3.9

Slightly longer than half of the shoulder seam
Figure 3.10 Strap.

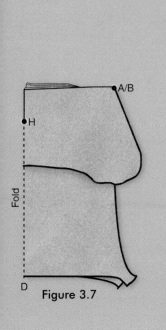

Figure 3.7

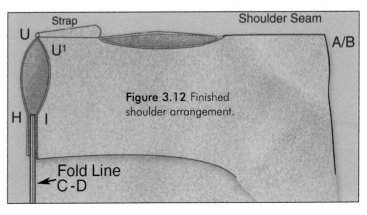

Figure 3.11

Figure 3.12 Finished shoulder arrangement.

Fold Line C-D

ADORNMENT OF THE SIDEFOLD DRESS

Old Sioux-style sidefold dresses are typically decorated with long lanes of painting, where a sizing medium was applied in narrow lanes to the hide before it was smoked. This left a whitish line against the smoky tan leather. Quillwork, which resembles the long narrow lane quillwork executed by members of the historic Cheyenne quillers' guilds, and/or beadwork in white or blue pony beads are always oriented horizontally on the dress, as in Figures 3.1 & 3.13. Lanes of adornment on the bottom half of the dress continue all the way around the dress, meeting smoothly so as to form single continuous lines. Lanes of adornment on the yoke are identically rendered on front and back of the dress.

The hemline of the sidefold dress was sometimes adorned with a row of metal cone tinklers, which lends a pleasing sound when walking through camp. A few of the historic sidefold garments also sport rows of small shells and/or brass buttons across the top of the yoke (see back cover), usually in conjunction with beaded elements. When adding decoration it is best to confine it to the yoke and lower half of the bodice, or area above the waist, avoiding the midriff area where your belt will be worn.

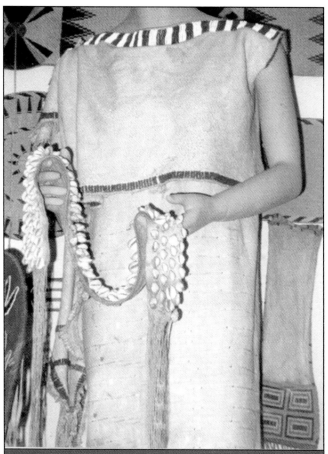

Figure 3.13. Sidefold dress from former Heye Foundation exhibit. Note horizontal orientation of decoration. National Museum of the American Indian, Washington, D.C. Photo by the author

SIOUX ACCESSORIES

Choosing the right accessories for the sidefold dress is quite a challenge. Very few primary sources even adequately describe the garment itself, let alone how it was worn, or what it was worn with. A Kurz sketch does show a Cree-type sidefold worn with a soft hide belt and close-fitting leggings (Feder 1984:55). Lewis & Clark's journal mentions Teton women wearing knee-length leather leggings, moccasins, and a hide robe (DeVoto, 1953:93). Appropriate accessories for the re-created sidefold dress might include: a soft hide belt of practical width, softsole moccasins of the sideseam style, close-fitting knee-high leggings made of leather, and a hide robe either painted or quilled. Remember, in terms of historical style, the sidefold dress is old, therefore the accessories you put with it should be correspondingly old, both in type and in decoration.

Feder guesses the Sioux style sidefold dress was worn with the side seam and bottom tab to the wear's left. He bases his guess primarily on the Karl Bodmer rendering "Teton Sioux Woman". Due to the fact that the woman has a large and beautiful painted robe wrapped around her shoulders, it is impossible to actually "see" the dress she is wearing. Only a portion of the hemline, including two tabs and an added flounce, is visible. This looks very similar to the hemline of Sioux-type sidefold dresses in museum collecions. If the woman painted by Bodmer is indeed wearing a sidefold dress, based on the location of the bottom tab on extant examples, she was wearing it with the fold to her right and the seam to her left.

Figure 3.14. Author's recreation of a woman's belt set from the mid-19th century. The soft hide belt and pouch with triangular flap are patterned after an original in the Masco Collection (page 45) and objects sketched by R.F. Kurz. The matching set, made from smoked elk, includes the ubiquitous awl case and woman's style knife sheath. Decorated with 8/0 beads in two shades of blue and white, tin cones, brass hawk bells and brass thimbles. Note the pleasing continuity of design elements.

SIOUX STYLE: Two-Hide Dress

To consider the Sioux two-hide dress is to get a fascinating glimpse at the evolution in style and adornment of a classic garment type. The construction of the Sioux two-hide dress varies from simple to complex, depending on the time period in question, the size of the hides available and the specific needs of the maker/wearer. As noted on page 13, Clark Wissler categorized three distinct sub-types of the two-hide dress. All three are encounteed within historic Sioux garments. Watch closely for them as we spend a moment looking at the history of the two-hide dresses worn by Sioux women.

Exactly when Sioux women began wearing the two-hide dress style is impossible to determine, but it undoubtedly is ancient. Descriptions contained in pre-1800 primary documents provide little conclusive information in this regard. However, by the first decade of the 19th century, first source material clearly reveals the two-hide dress as the predominantly Sioux style. According to Tabeau (1939:145), whose journal dates from 1802-1803, Sioux two-hide dresses of this time period were being made from elk, deer, or antelope skins, and sported lengthy fringe along the hem, side seams, and sleeve areas. However, he may have observed incorrectly, as mountain sheep were most generally used and antelope hides would have been used for smaller examples only. Tabeau also noted porcupine quillwork as the typical ornamental addition to these dresses. The journals of Lewis & Clark (1804) mentions the length of Sioux dresses as being almost to the ankles. Both accounts cite belts worn with the dresses.

Most old two-hide dresses retain the leg pendants and crescent curves of the hemline. In fact, in many cases these are even exaggerated or enhanced. The bottom section of the dress is always very full. Such fullness is a practical necessity: women rode horseback yet needed to maintain an acceptable level of modesty. Arthur Amiotte comments, "when a woman rode a horse, and I observed my grandmother doing this, she would pull her dress up and foreword between her legs before mounting. Then she would rearrange this long part to cover her legs, out of modesty" (Batkin, 1995:28). Of course, this is out of necessity as well, in order to be able to sit on the horse. A robe or blanket was often folded and placed over the lap and legs.

By the 1830s, Sioux two-hide garments for dress-up occasions were being "decorated with bands of quills or beads along the outer seams of the sleeves, across the neck, over the seam attaching the

Figure 3.15 Probably Sioux, collected prior to 1855 by the Indian agent, Thomas S. Twiss, this fine dress is decorated in pony beads, embellished with genuine elk teeth and the mountain sheep tail which has been left intact at the neck. The tail is accentuated by undulating lanes of blue beadwork which follow the contour of the yoke, a characteristic of Sioux dresses two decades later. Length 107 cm. Courtesy National Museum of the American Indian, Washington, D.C., Catalog No. 5.3776

yoke to the dress, and around the hemline" (Markoe, 1986:75). Maximilian described one Sioux dress with "stripes and borders of azure and white beads and polished metal buttons, and trimmed as usual at the bottom with fringes, round the ends of which lead is twisted so that they tinkle at every motion" (Maximilian, 1906:213). Two Catlin portraits, "Ychon-su-mons-ka" (Sand Bar - Sioux wife of Francis Chardon) and "Wi-looh-tah-eeh-tchah-ta-mah-nee" (Red Thing That Touches in Marching) are particularly revealing. Both of the women are portrayed wearing dresses with a lane of beadwork along the top of the sleeve/shoulder area. The yoke of Sand Bar's dress, which is clearly shown with the tail and edge of hair of the animal hide intact, is totally covered with small brass buttons. Although the portrait of Red Thing That Touches in Marching does not show a contoured yoke, the yoke area is decorated with two rows of brass buttons parallel to the neck opening (Catlin, 1973:Plates 94 and 95). See Figures 3.16 and 3.17.

By the mid 1800s, beaded elements on the two-hide dress were no longer just simple bands. Soon the entire yoke of special occasion dresses was being covered with lane-stitch beadwork in "pony"-size beads. Simultaneously with this decorative elaboration was the development of the Type-3 two-hide dress. This style offered the craftworkers a much larger uninterrupted field on which to bead. The beaded areas on mid-1800 Sioux dress tops are nearly always solid light to medium light blue, bordered by a single lane of contrasting color along the edges and across the shoulders and neck, while the very earliest Sioux yokes are white background.

By the latter half of the 19th century the entire upper portion of a woman's dress-up garment might be covered in lane-stitch seed beadwork. Fully beaded Lakota dresses from this period typically have a blue background enclosed by a three-lane-wide multi-colored border. Instead of an actual tail, the yoke area on these Lakota dresses had a vestigial U-shape design worked in beads. Referred to as a turtle or lizard, this beaded motif was said to resemble 'the t'elanuwe' or "umbilical containers made for newborns". Worn only by women, this motif was thought to provide the wearer with "protection against female disorders and diseases" (Powers, 1986:86).

Other geometric figures were typically beaded within the larger blue field. Tradition says that when a woman wore this style of dress it identified her with "the earth and the waters" (Batkin, 1995:28).

Figure 3.16. Sketch of dress top shown in Catlin portait of Red Thing that Touches in Marching.

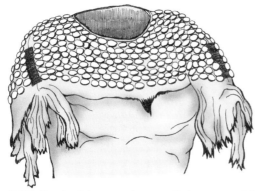

Figure 3.17. Sketch of dress top shown in Catlin portrait of Sand Bar.

Figure 3.18. "The Rush Gatherer", a classic example of a Plains two-hide tail dress, undoubtedly of mountain sheep. Note how the hair on the mountain sheep tail is trimmed short. Photo reproduced from the Collections of the Library of Congress, No. USZ62-7721.

"DEER" TAIL DRESSES:
Fact or Fiction
by Wes Housler

The two hide dress hit it's peak in popularity and was most wide spread before 1850. During this time, especially before the great migration of white settlers to the west coast in the early '40's, bighorn sheep were quite plentiful. Today we consider mountain sheep habitat synonymous with the Rocky Mountains, but in fact sheep once lived all over the Great Plains, anywhere there was a little 'badland' country.

Old journals record sheep as far east as Scotts Bluff in western Nebraska, thus making them accessible to any of the Central Plains tribes. Gilbert Wilson recorded in his notes on the Hidasta, when hunting sheep that, "Bighorn skins, when obtained, were not only handled with greater care than were hides from other animals, but the method of transporting them differed." [Weitzner 1979, p. 196] The tribes along the upper Missouri hunted sheep in South and North Dakota along the river breaks and any other rough, broken stretches of land.

Osbourne Russell, who was in the West from 1834-1843, had this to say about sheep hides: "The skins when dressed are softer and far superior to those of the Deer for clothing. It is of them that the Squaws make their dresses" [Russell, 1986:34l].

Historically, the majority of two-hide dresses were made from bighorn sheep. I do not know of any made from deer but I have identified a couple made from elk. Currently most museum catalogs are incorrectly identifying this style of dress and most pre-1850 shirts as deer when in fact they are sheep.

The first modern reference to this appears in **Yupika: The Plains Indian Woman's Dress** (Taylor, 1997:51), in the form of a comparison sketch and description by Bill Holm.

I've been fortunate enough to have brain-tanned a half dozen sheep hides over the years and have found them to be quite strong, but with a light to medium weight and thickness. They remind me of an antelope except they are much larger, with a mature ram weighing in at over 300 pounds.

The problem with using deer for a dress is that it takes two abnormally large deer, which are hard to find, and once found they are thick and heavy. This is why elk were utilized, especially in the later years after sheep were hunted out. By fall a calf elk is larger than any deer, with the exception being your monster buck. But because of its younger age the skin will tan out quite thin making for a lightweight dress. The problem with elk is that it doesn't have that bright white hair along its back legs.

Rather than going on with more boring quotes to prove this point I hope you'll study the two photographs, 3.19 and 3.20, at left and compare them to Bodmer's paintings or any museum dress that still has the tail and hair attached. The short dark tail with white hair extending down the legs is the marking of a sheep, not a mule deer nor black-tailed deer.

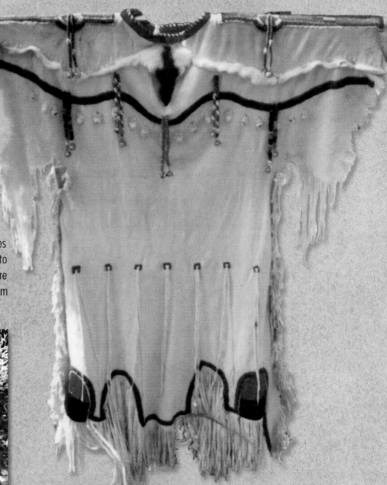

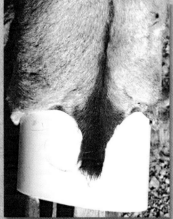

Figure 3.19 (left) Bighorn sheep tail, short with dark hair.

Figure 3.20 (right) Mule deer hide with white tail at least twice a long as sheep

Figure 3.21 An excellent example of the Sioux style two-hide dress as re-created by the author. Note the scalloping along the bottom of the dress and the added tail. Other recognizable features of all Sioux style dresses are the soft leather ties and the addition of elk teeth that adorn this dress. Photo courtesy of Wes Housler.

CONSTRUCTION

As mentioned on page 13, the Type-3 two-hide dress is technically almost a three-hide dress. Instead of a narrow self-yoke, the Type-3 garment has a wide rectangular-shaped yoke made from an additional hide. The Type-3 two-hide dress, however, retains the deeply undulating "natural" hemline of the Type-1 and Type-2 dresses, rather than being straight-cut like the classic three-hide dress of the Southern Plains. The characteristic undulated hem probably defines the Type-3 garment as an evolutionary form of the basic two-hide style.

The yoke of the Type-3 two-hide dress has no natural contour or tail tuft where it joins the dress body front and back. Instead, the stylistic form of the Type-3 two-hide dress relies on the beaded imitation of these features. The yoke is decorated with lane-stitch beadwork in gently undulating horizontal lanes — which would imitate the contours of the butt ends of the hides if they had been folded down as in the Type-1 dress. Central to this imitative feature is a sharp downward curve in the middle of the beaded lanes. This is a beaded representation of the tail, based on where it would lie on the yoke of a Type-1 garment. Coupled with the deeply undulating hemline, these beadwork characteristics (undulating lanes plus a sharp central downcurve) give the Type-3 dress it's distinct look.

Having said this, what does it mean for the craftsperson trying to re-create such a garment? Simply put...if one intends to create a viably historic Type 3 two-hide dress for use at a rendezvous or powwow, just cutting the leather to the required dimensions and sewing up the dress won't do it. The two characteristics (pattern and adornment) put together are what

make the Type-3 two-hide dress unique. Therefore, doing the beadwork is a must. I encourage you to look at as many pictures of originals as possible, so that you can make informed decisions about the lay-out and overall appearance of the beadwork. You should do this study before undertaking any construction project. Why? Because the best time to do the beadwork on this type of garment is at certain specific times during the construction process itself.

MATERIALS

For creating a Sioux-style Type-3 two-hide dress, you will need to acquire at least four large deer hides (for the average-framed woman). These hides should be big enough that when you hold them butt-end-up to yourself, they appear proportioned to your body in height and width, with space to spare. If you cannot find deer hides of the necessary size, consider purchasing elk hides instead. At least two of these hides should have the requisite "from-the-animal" shape, similar to the bold outline in Figures 3.22 and 3.23, or they should be large enough that you can cut them into a correct shape yourself. This is necessary for achieving the outline of the skirt piece illustrated in Figure 3.23. Purchase several additional hides of the same color if you plan to make matching accessories. Remember, if you will be working with commercially tanned leather, you must take care in assembly of the garment in order to retain continuity between texture (i.e., all hides "rough side out").

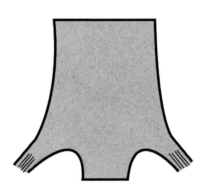

Figure 3.23 Body piece.

In addition to the leather requirements stated above, you will need the following construction supplies for this dress project: heavy-duty scissors, measuring tape, yard stick and ruler, seamstress' chalk, heavy duty straight pins, an awl or a large glover's -needle, artificial sinew, 12"x12" pieces of dark red and royal blue wool felt, fabric glue (optional), and a large well-lit work space.

MEASUREMENTS

To create a Type-3 two-hide dress you will need to have the following measurements of the intended wearer:

1. Waist (plus 4-6").
2. Hips (plus 4-6").
3. Elbow-to-elbow, across the shoulders & neck.
4. Top of shoulder to 2" below armpit.
5. Armpit to armpit, across the bustljne.
6. Armpit to back-of-the-knee/mid-calf.

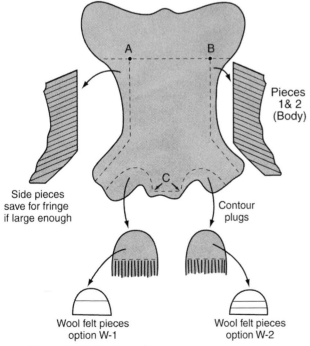

Side pieces save for fringe if large enough

Contour plugs

A   B

Pieces 1 & 2 (Body)

C

Wool felt pieces option W-1

Wool felt pieces option W-2

Figure 3.22 Contour plugs

THREE BASIC DRESS PIECES

With these measurements, use a yardstick or a ruler to mark the hides with the dimensions of the three large pieces which make up this garment. You will have two identical body pieces like that shown in Figure 3.23, and one yoke piece like that shown in Figure 3.24. They are taken from three hides as laid out in Figure 3.22. For Body Pieces 1 & 2, the distance between Points A and B equals measurement #5 (armpit to armpit, across the bustline). The distance between Line A-B, and Line C is measurement #6 (armpit to back-of-the-knee/mid-calf). Use seamstress chalk and/or pins to mark the dimensions out on one hide.

Special note about "body " fringe: If you are working with large enough hides, clearly mark the hemline (bottom edge of the shirt) dimensions with chalk, but leave a few inches of leather below it. This can be cut into self-fringe later. The two ""tabs" on the bottom of each side of Body Pieces 1 & 2 can also be left extra long if your hide-space allows for it. This extra leather can also be cut into fringe later. If the hides are not large enough, you will need to save a swatch of leather equal in length to Line C, and two small swatches of leather the width of the "'tabs" (six total swatches per dress.). Sew these pieces in place (be careful to match leather texture.). You can cut them into fringes later, after the dress is decorated. Also, if it's wide enough, you should save the excess leather along the sides of each body piece. These can then be cut into fringe which will be inserted later during the side seam construction of the dress. Do not leave these pieces attached to the leather. Just cut them out and save them. Take a moment to fringe them if you wish, then set them aside.

Dress Body- Remember to measure and cut the first "body" piece with the rough texture of the leather facing you. If the two hides you are using for these "body" pieces are of relatively equal size and shape, you can use your already-cut-out Piece 1 as a pattern for marking out the dimensions on Piece 2. Here's how. After you have cut Piece l out, lay the second hide flat with the rough side of the leather up and use Piece 1 momentarily flipped over so the slick side is up, to lay on top of it. Be sure you are stacking the hides with appropriate ends matching. Now, trace around "Body" Piece 1 to get the dimensions for Piece 2, which you can then cut out. You should now have two identical "body" pieces, shaped roughly like that shown in Figure 3.23. If you are leaving excess leather in place along Line C for fringing later, the dimensions of your "body" pieces will look slightly different for now.

Yoke- For Piece 3 (shown in Figure 3.24) which will be the "yoke" of the finished dress, Lines D-D1 and E-E1 are measurement #4 (top of shoulder to 2" below armpit), and Lines D-E and D1-E1 are measurement #3 (elbow-to-elbow across the shoulders and neck). Use your measurements from Pieces 1 & 2 to note Points A, B, , and B1 on Piece 3, too. These are superimposed on Lines D-E and D1-E1 as shown in Figure 3.25. Layout the dimensions as shown in Figure 3.25, taking care that your measurements are correctly lined up so as to produce the requisite rectangular shape. Mark the dimensions clearly with seamstress chalk and/or pins.

Special note about "yoke" fringe (shown in Figure 3.27): If the hide you are working with for this "yoke" piece is large enough to leave more than five to six inches of extra leather between Lines D-D1 and E-E1 along the edges of the hide, you can simply mark these lines and leave the excess leather, which can be cut to create the "sleeve" fringe. If there is no excess to work with, you will need to save two large sections of leather, roughly rectangular and as long as dimensions D-D1 and E-E1, which should be cut for fringe and carefully sewn onto the yoke along "sleeve" Lines D-D1 and E-E1. Remember to correctly match hide texture.

Cut out Piece 3. This is the yoke piece shown in Figure 3.27. If the hide was large enough for you to leave excess for self-fringe, the dimension of your rectangle will look slightly different for now. Fringe the excess if you wish – or you may wait until after the dress decoration is complete.

CONTOUR PLUGS

The next step in the creation of a Type-3 two-hide dress is the creation and insertion of the "contour" plugs in the deep plunges along the hemline. Basically these plugs are large U-shaped panels, with the lower portion cut into fringe and the upper portion ornamented with pieces of wool tradecloth. You will need to make four of these plugs, and therefore will need four large pieces of leather. The excess leather from the butt end of the hides which is left over from cutting out Body Pieces 1 & 2 should be more than enough.

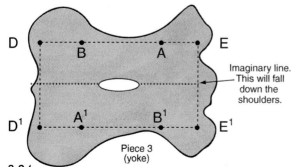

Figure 3.24

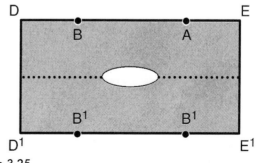

Figure 3.25

Chapter 3: Central Plains Dresses

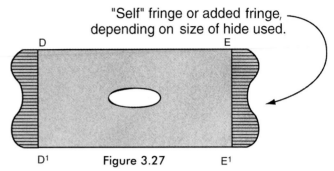

"Self" fringe or added fringe, depending on size of hide used.

D   E

D¹   Figure 3.27   E¹

Use your already-cut dress body pieces as visual guides for getting the correct dimensions for the inverted "U" shape, but remember to leave an extra quarter inch or so along the rounded portion as a seam allowance if these plugs will be sewn into place in the hemline plunges. These plugs can also be very simply laced in place, as was done on numerous original dresses. Lay the body pieces atop the leather you are using for the plugs with the rough side of all leather facing up, and trace the curving contour. Lay aside the body pieces. Now it is a simple matter to just continue drawing the lines for the sides of the "U" straight downward on each side of the curve. This creates the requisite "U" shape.

The "U" should be long enough that the plug will project two to three inches below Line C when the plug is sewn into place. Cut out the four plugs – but not before somehow identifying each plug with the plunge into which it fits, so you can correctly match these up later. Yes, it really does make a difference. I often use dress-makers pins with the colored ball heads for this identification process, using like-colored pinheads to delineate which plug matches which plunge.

Historical dresses from museum collections as well as those shown in paintings by Bodmer and Catlin reveal many different methods of decorating these contour plugs, so there is a bit of latitude in your choice. Most of the primary examples feature a piece of red tradewool, often alongside a contrasting color piece, typically a very dark blue. These fabric pieces are often accompanied by ornamental leather thonging and/or beadwork. On any given dress, all four plugs will be identically adorned.

The typical layout of the woolen pieces is shown in Figure 3.28 and Figure 3.33. This illustrates several different orientation options for these pieces. The wool pieces are sewn into place with small basting stitches. A lane of decorative running stitch done using a long narrow leather thong is often added along the edges of the wool pieces. This is ornamental as well as practical reinforcement of the attachment. One of these lanes of running stitch can cover the line formed where two different colors of woolen fabric meet – or this line can be covered by a narrow lane of white lazy stitch beadwork 2-3 beads wide. For added reinforcement when attaching the fabric pieces to the leather plugs, you can also use a bit of fabric glue. Use it sparingly, and spread it evenly to avoid potential ripples or clumping when the woolcloth is dry.

When you have completed the decoration on the four U-shaped plugs, you can sew them into place in the appropriate contour plunges which you marked earlier. Working from the back side, with the slick texture of the leather facing you, pin the top of the U in place first. Work out from this center point, pinning until the U-shape takes its downward turn away from the edges of the contour. Don't pin too much. The bottom 2/3 of the sides of the "U" will not be attached to the dress. The plug should hang down freely from the dress, not causing the hemline to bunch up in any way.

Figure 3.26. An example of the typical Sioux style, two-hide dress as re-created by the author. Note the scalloping along the bottom of the dress and the added tail. Other recognizable features of all Sioux style dresses are the soft leather ties and the addition of elk teeth or cowrie shells that adorn this dress. Photo by the author.

Figure 3.28 Close-up example of a contour plug. Photo by the author.

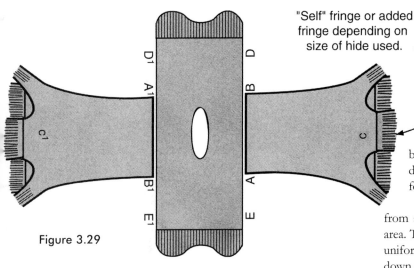

Figure 3.29

"Self" fringe or added fringe depending on size of hide used.

After pinning, use artificial sinew and two sharp glovers needles to sew the plugs into place in the contours. Working from the back side and beginning at the top, use small tight over-and-over stitches to sew down over one side of the curve using one half of your thread. The other half- left hanging -will be used to sew down over the other side of the curve. Press the edges of the leather together gently, but keep your stitches very small so that the seam puckers upward only slightly. Using the second needle attached to the other half of the thread, you should also begin sewing down the other side of the curve. Alternate back and forth between threads/sides. Again, do not sew too far down. Stop occasionally and hold up the dress piece you're working on, allowing it to hang as if it were being worn. If the top of the contour is bunching, or the plug isn't hanging down freely along the sides of the "U", you have sewn too much and need to remove a few stitches. When everything hangs down neatly, with the hemline remaining flat, you can tie off the ends of the thread securely.

DECORATION

It is much easier to decorate this garment before the three main pieces are completely assembled. I recommend beginning with the two body pieces. As with your garment's historic counterparts, the front and the back should be identically decorated. Type-3 dresses from the early-to-middle 19th century typically have a single row of lane stitch beadwork flowing along the entire length of the hem, plus a number of accompanying ornamental beadwork figures in squares or triangles, and adornment thongs. I recommend attaching the thongs before doing the beading, because they can be used as visual guides for the placement of beadwork and because the small beaded squares or triangles are often worked right over the attachment point of the thongs, effectively hiding them. (See Figure 3.34)

Lay out "Body" Pieces 1 & 2 side-by-side. Scrutinize them closely and decide how and where you want the adornment thongs. Plan to attach them in as symmetrical a pattern as possible. Work with the natural curves of the two pieces, rather than against them. Much of the beauty of the Type-3 two-hide dress lies in its elegant flowing form, tastefully enhanced by simplicity in adornment. The idea is not to overdo the decorative elements. Figure 3.34 offers two lay-out suggestions for the placement of the thongs and the beadwork with them.

Decorative thongs can be cut from excess leather, preferably from a thicker portion of the hide, rather than a thinner flank area. They should be narrow (no wider than 1/8 th of an inch), of uniform thickness, tapering to a point, and long enough to hang down at least four to five inches after they are attached, dampened and gently stretched as described in Chapter 1. The thongs should be attached to the dress as shown in Figure 3.34. When you are finished attaching all the thongs on Pieces 1 & 2, you can proceed with beadwork.

BEADWORK CONSIDERATIONS

In order to assure that the finished dress has the period look you wish to achieve, choose beads that are of historically appropriate color and size. The beads used during this period were Italian, and the colors were quite different than those available in the modern Czech beads. Therefore, one should use the old-time bead colors that are being reproduced today in order to more closely approximate the beads

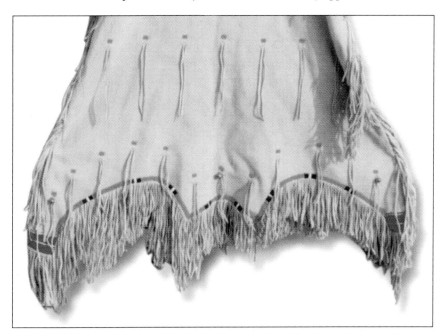

Figure 3.30 Lower half of author's re-creation of a Sioux, Type-2 two hide dress from the 19th century (National Museum of the American Indian Collections). This garment required three large elk hides, two for the body and one for the yoke. 8/0 beadwork is in sky blue, cobalt blue and white. Accents include tradecloth pieces, faux elk teeth and brass hawk bells. Note the gentler hemline contour. This dress is identical front and back. Photo by the author.

Chapter 3: Central Plains Dresses

from this period. On most historic examples, the beadwork is done primarily in blue. This is not a bold navy blue, but the softer muted "greasy" blues of old stock beads, such as "pony trader", "powder" or "Bodmer" blue. A few limited secondary bead colors are also seen on historic examples, including white, dark navy blue, black (except Sioux), red and green. However, white is by far the most common secondary color and even the old time white was different than the modern white. Other colors are used sparingly...only as accents. The beadwork on Type-3 two-hide dresses is typically executed in pony size beads, roughly equivalent in size to the modern size 8/0 pony beads. Lanes are typically anywhere from five to nine beads in width. The beadwork technique used is lane stitch. The beadwork on the average Type-3 two-hide dress will require 1½ to 2 kilos of the primary color, and several hanks of any supplementary color. Be sure to purchase more beads than you think you will need.

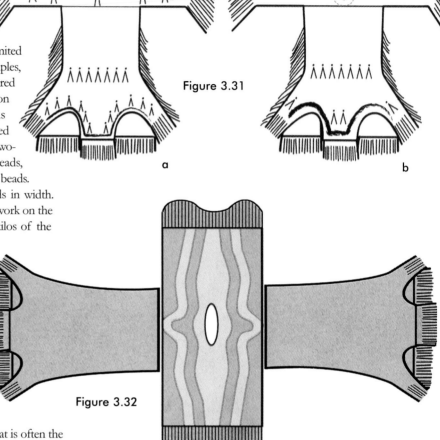

Figure 3.31

Figure 3.32

BEADWORK ON THE BODY PIECES

The easiest lane of beadwork to do is the one along the hemline. Basically you're just following the hem contours across the bottom of the dress, front and back. This lane is actually quite important to the look of the finished garment, defining the flowing lines and highlighting them. As strange as this may sound, I have found that it is this lane of beadwork that is often the most directly noticeable when the dress is being worn, particularly when there is a strong dark bead/light-colored leather contrast. The eyes are drawn to it as the garment sways and flows with its wearer's movements. I have heard it said that the older historic dress styles are most beautiful when "moving", and I tend to agree.

After finishing this lane of lazy stitch beadwork along the hemline of both body pieces, complete the decoration of these two pieces by adding the small triangular or square beaded figures just above or over the top of the adornment thongs, as illustrated in Figure 3.34. Choose a color layout that will enhance the overall continuity of the garment. Don't overdo the use of secondary bead colors. Also, pay special attention to the accuracy of the vertical orientation of these little figures. If just one is slightly askew, it will be the one that gets noticed. Work carefully and with precision. Refer to Figure 3.32 for the "look" of these figures.

ATTACHING BODY TO YOKE

Before doing the beadwork on the yoke of the dress, you must attach the two body pieces to the yoke. Why? Because the beadwork elements on the yoke – especially the central downcurving motif – will require more vertical space than the yoke piece itself allows and therefore of necessity may extend downward just a bit into the very upper portions of the body pieces. Working with the hides flipped

so the slick side is toward you, center Line A-B of Piece I on Line D-E of the Yoke (Piece 3) and sew the two together using artificial sinew and a tight over-and-over stitch. Do the same for Line A1-B1 of Piece 1 on Line D1-E1 of the yoke (Piece 3). See Figure 3.29 for this layout, and Figure 3.31 for the completed look.

YOKE BEADWORK

With the partially completed garment lying as in Figure 3.30, it is now time to concentrate your decorative efforts on the yoke of the dress. Your careful study of historic examples and primary artwork will prepare you to choose a pattern/design that is historically viable and coordinates tastefully with the beadwork already executed on Pieces 1 & 2. You must then transfer this idea into concrete form, laying out the pattern carefully on your unfinished dress. Use white seamstress' chalk or light pencilmarks, pins or whatever you are comfortable with to mark this pattern on your dress yoke, both front and back. Be careful using pins, especially with commercial hide, as they will leave pinholes.

I have found it helpful to begin the beadwork on the yoke by starting with the lane that extends from each side of the neck opening outward to the middle of the end of the "sleeves". This is your "centering" lane, and must be executed precisely. Once

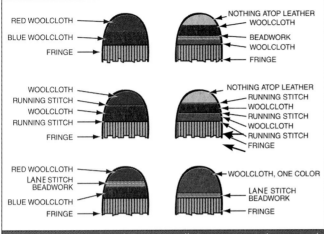

Figure 3.33 These patches are usually cut square at the top and the shape of the hide causes them to appear rounded as shown.

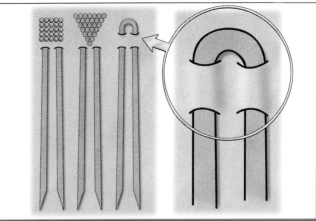

Figure 3.34. Attaching thongs.& bead decorations. A small square or disc of red wool can be skewered by the thongs for additional decoration.

Figure 3.35 Example of beadwork on the yoke, Sioux style, ca. 1830. *Photograph by the author.*

this lane is correctly in place, you will find it much easier to keep all the other subsequent lanes straight and symmetrical. If the garment you are creating is to have a solid area of beadwork over the upper portion of the yoke, you should complete this solidly beaded portion in it's entirety before beading any separate lanes beneath it. By finishing the upper yoke section first, you will have a visual guide for laying out additional lanes. The lower edge of the yoke section in both front and back should exhibit the characteristic, gentle undulation. Use this undulating wave as your visual orientation for beading additional lanes, which also undulate, below it. When the dress is laid out flat on the floor as in Figure 3.32, the undulations will resemble waves lapping on a beach.

Choose your overall pattern carefully so it is balanced and symmetrical. Remember that although the lane-stitch beadwork produces vertically stacked beads in the stitches which make up each lane, the beaded lanes themselves are always oriented horizontally. This creates a strong – and quite stunning – visual impression. Once the yoke area beadwork is complete, continue with assembly of the dress.

FINISHING TOUCHES

Picking the dress up, wrong side out, at the shoulders, align armpit Points A & B', and A' & B. With a long piece of reserved "fringe" leather sandwiched between, sew up each side, beginning at the armpit points and working downward toward the bottom edge. Pinch the three layers together tightly, keeping the edges even. Either use an awl to pierce holes before sewing, or use a glovers needle with artificial sinew to sew these seams up, leaving a quarter inch seam allowance. Using a running stitch technique, take small tight stitches. Throw in an occasional backstitch for added seam strength and durability. This also helps to keep the seam flat. Stop sewing when you reach the outward curve of the "tab" projections. Securely tie off the thread.

Turn the dress right side out. If you have not already done so, attach and/or cut the fringe along the edges of the hemline, hem tabs, and "sleeves". Your Type-3 two-hide dress is now finished.

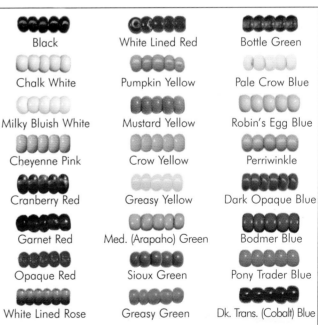

Black	White Lined Red	Bottle Green
Chalk White	Pumpkin Yellow	Pale Crow Blue
Milky Bluish White	Mustard Yellow	Robin's Egg Blue
Cheyenne Pink	Crow Yellow	Perriwinkle
Cranberry Red	Greasy Yellow	Dark Opaque Blue
Garnet Red	Med. (Arapaho) Green	Bodmer Blue
Opaque Red	Sioux Green	Pony Trader Blue
White Lined Rose	Greasy Green	Dk. Trans. (Cobalt) Blue

Figure 3.36 Old Time Bead Colors - A limited range of colors was available to the early beadworker, with these being the most common. Note: These identifying color names are generally accepted among craftworker-collector-researcher community. Photo courtesy of Crazy Crow Trading Post

Chapter 3: Central Plains Dresses

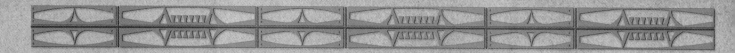

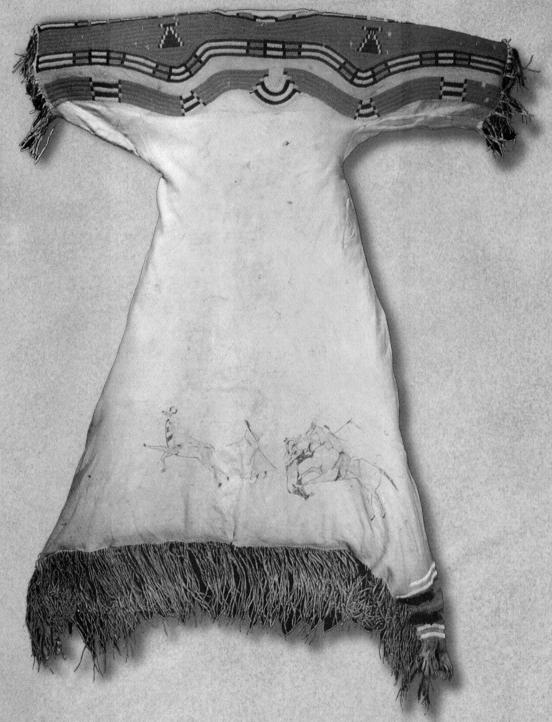

Figure 3.37 Hunkpapa Lakota Pictographic Dress, ca. 1875. Collected by David Toro at Standing Rock, North Dakota. The sleeve ends are not typical Lakota, but could be an early version of the truly rectangular yokes of Northern Sioux, ca. 1900. This dress is adorned with lane-stitch beadwork (medium blue being the dominant color), small tin cones, and two groups of painted hunting scenes front and back. The combination of beadwork with drawings is an unusual feature on dresses. It is probable that the figures of the hunters, who have a female appearance, could be "winkte" (berdaches) or two-spirit people. It is unknown whether the dressmaker was one of the persons represented by the figures in the paintings. Courtesy of State Historical Society of North Dakota, Photo No. L641.

19th Century Plains Indian Dresses

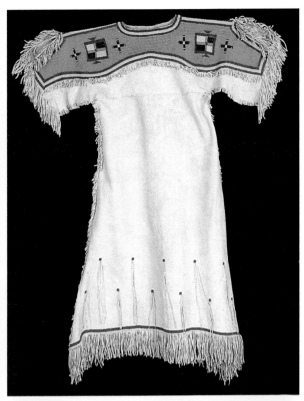

Figure 3.39 Sioux Woman's Dress, ca. 1890. The rather compact, square beaded designs on this dress represent a transitional phase from the simple designs of the early period of beadwork to the more intricate designs of the late reservation style. Of interest is the somewhat unusual treatment of additional fringe along the bottom edge of the yoke. Constructed of tanned hide with fringed sleeves, side seams, and bottom edge. Yoke is fully beaded with seed beads in light blue background, with design elements in red, greasy yellow, light blue and dark blue, with its bottom margin and ends of its sleeves retaining somewhat the outline of classic, whole skin dress yokes. Photo courtesy of Morning Star Gallery.

Figure 3.38 (Above) Sioux hide dress with magnificent, fully beaded yoke, ca. 1880. Note the unusual pink background color and multiple lanes of beadwork along the bottom edge and tin cones on the side tabs. Chicago Field Museum display. Courtesy of Written Heritage Collection. Photo by Joe Kazumura.

Figure 3.40 Sioux Dress, ca. 1880. The fully beaded yoke of this fine dress is a sky blue background with white and white-lined red accents. In the middle of the yoke, the upward undulation of the white outlining lanes is reminiscent of the location of the downward pointing "tail" on the yokes of earlier garments. Of note is the minimal adornment on the lower portions of this dress, which is somewhat uncommon for any era. Field Museum of Natural History, Chicago. Photo courtesy of Maj. Gen. Michael C. Kostelnik USAF (Ret). Photo by Michael Kostelnik.

Chapter 3: Central Plains Dresses

Figure 3.41 Sioux Girl's Dress, ca. 1890. Tanned hide with fully beaded yoke in early classic style. Fully beaded yoke in light blue background seed beads with U-shaped bib reminiscent of residual tail of the animal. Edging is in matching light blue color. 40" W x 45"L.
Courtesy Morning Star Gallery, Photo No.19587.

SIOUX Accessories

TYPE-3 TWO-HIDE DRESS

Accessories to be worn with the Sioux-style, Type-3 two-hide dress should include four basic items: moccasins, leggings, belt and robe. Sioux women's moccasins and leggings from the early-to-mid 19th. century were separate items, not the one-piece "boot". The predominant moccasin style from this time period was the side-seam, not the hard-sole. Simple tubular leggings can be made from leather or from blue or red tradecloth.

Moccasins and leggings with matching decoration are particularly striking and can add significantly to the overall "finished" appearance of an outfit. If the beaded patterns on these accessories also coordinate with the beadwork on the dress itself, the effect is even more stunning, but be careful not to color-coordinate too much as this is a modern trait. Decoration should be kept simple. Just a touch of quillwork or beadwork (single lanes, small triangles, narrow bars – done in pony size beads) placed primarily over seams, atop the moccasin toes, and over the seams and along the bottom edges of the leggings, is all the adornment necessary.

Without a belt, the dress is incomplete (Markoe, 1986:75). Historic evidence from the early-to-mid-1800's, the time frame of the classic two-hide dress, indicates that women's belts were commonly made from soft tanned leather or from rawhide. Re-creating the soft leather belt is simple enough. Calculate the length of the belt by measuring the wearer's waist and multiplying this number by 2. Doing this allows plenty of length for tying the ends securely together, then letting them hang downward. Cut a one to two inch wide strip of sturdy elk or bison hide to the necessary length. The ends can be fringed, widened into a "tab" style, pinked, or left blunt. It is also good to get the "stretch" out of a belt as well.

Soft hide belts can be left plain or adorned with touches of beadwork or quillwork, if desired, especially the pendant ends. I suggest studying the paintings of Karl Bodmer (Maximilian, 1906). If you pay close attention to the belts you will get a good feel for historically appropriate styles and decorations. These soft hide belts were normally worn tied in the front. In order to help keep the trailing ends out of lapwork or any project the wearer undertakes when kneeling or stooping, they can be tucked up under the belt temporarily. Various accessories can (and should be) attached to the

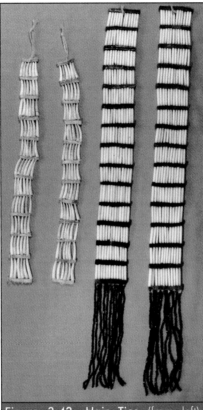

Figure 3.42 Hair Ties (from left): Sioux hair ties of dentalium shells (antique). Arapaho (possibly) hair ties of white bugle beads and faceted black beads (antique, restrung). Courtesy of Benson Lanford collection. Photo by Benson Lanford.

belt. These might include a knife in its sheath, an awl in its case, and a small pouch, like those illustrated on page 50, for toting flint-and-steel.

A belt made from rawhide should be cut from good quality hide of medium thickness. If the rawhide is too thin, the belt will fold and bend too much, eventually rippling in an unsightly and uncomfortable manner. A rawhide belt should be cut to the exact dimension of the wearer's waist. Two sets of sturdy soft leather tie thongs should be attached to each end. These meet when the belt is wrapped around the wearer, and are tied to secure the belt in place. Holes that will stay open in rawhide are generally made by piercing, wetting and inserting a pointed dowel, which is left in the hole until the hide dries.

Belts made from heavy harness leather adorned with brass tacks are also historically accurate for this time period (Jennys, 1995:11-14). Extra wide belts covered with lots of tacks are a later, 19th. century style, more characteristic of the Northern Plains look, and therefore should probably be avoided as an accessory for a Sioux-style look. Further, belts adorned with German silver disks or south-western styled conchos are also to be avoided because these items also invoke a late 19th century look. However, brass was available at this time and in limited use.

Trade blankets and hide robes are both appropriate choices for outerwear; however, a blanket coat or capote is not (Jennys, 1993:33-35). Select a blanket that is historic in style, material and color. Be sure to choose a blanket color that compliments the overall appearance of your outfit, rather than working against it. Wear the blanket draped over your shoulders and wrapped around your body. It requires no beaded decoration. Wide beaded "blanket strips" were not common until the latter half of the 1800's.

Beautifully tanned hide robes are elegant by themselves and can be left plain. However, a carefully painted or quilled robe, worn correctly, can be a spectacular compliment to an outfit. The most common painted design on Sioux women's robes was the box-and-border. It is seen on the robe worn by Bodmer's subject in his famous painting "Teton Sioux Woman". An example of this box-and-border pattern, as reproduced by the author, is shown in Figure 3.46.

Chapter 3: Central Plains Dresses

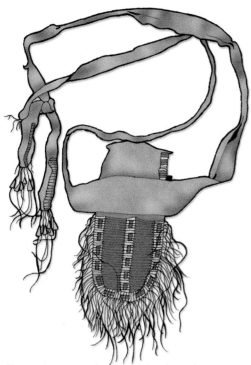

Figure 3.43 Another example of a soft-hide belt with a belt bag, ca. 1840. This pouch is beaded in pony beads and is heavily fringed. The belt has ornamental tin cones added to the ends and is sinew sewn. Tucker Collection, Cat. No. A6241. Illustration by Jessica Reddick.

Figure 3.44 Sioux Woman's Moccasins - This pair (circa 1880) is ornamented with beadwork and quillwork with designs, colors and layout typical of classic Lakota women's moccasins. The bottom portion of the wearer's leggings would extend to the tops of the moccasins proper, covering the undecorated ankle extensions which are somewhat unusual in that they are made of cloth rather than hide. Courtesy Richard Green Collection, UK. Photo by Richard Green.

Figure 3.45 Strike-a-light bag, ca. 1870. Native-tanned hide, glass beads, tin cones. Bag for fire steel, tinder and flintstone. Heinz Bründl Collection, photo courtesy Robert Wagner.

Figure 3.46 Author's re-creation of woman's robe from the first half of the 19th Century. This "Box and Border" pattern was interpreted from an original in the Wied Collection and is also the pattern which was worn by the subject in Bodmers painting "Teton Sioux Woman" (see painting on page 1). Historically, robes were worn on a horizontal orientation, with the head of the animal wrapping around the wearer's left side. Photo by the author.

Figure 3.47 Two fine, beaded Awl Cases or Hair-Parter Cases from the Benson Lanford Collection. The one on the left is possibly Kiowa-Apache, while the one on the right is Sioux. Courtesy Benson Lanford Collection. Photo by Benson Lanford

19th Century Plains Indian Dresses

Figure 3.48 Dentalium Shell Saved-List Cloth Dress – This fine example, formerly in the June Poitras collection, is undoubtedly Sioux. It was restored by Tom Murphy for his wife, Karel. Made of blue saved-list cloth, it is an excellent example of the heavy use of dentalium shells by the Sioux. It is further decorated with brass sequins and red and light blue ribbon. Note the creative placement of the dentalium and sequins that form circular and tipi shaped designs on the sleeves and along the bottom edge of the dress. Karel Murphy Collection. Photo courtesy of Tom Murphy.

Chapter 3: Central Plains Dresses

SIOUX STYLE: Tradecloth Dress

When speaking chronologically about the material aspects of Lakota culture, the wearing of cloth dresses is often associated only with the latter half of the 19th century. This is truly unfortunate, because it is possible to trace trade-cloth dresses in Lakota history before 1800. Rosemary Lessard asserts that the Lakota "had cloth early in their history and were using it before they became Plains people." (Lessard, 1980:72.) Traders' inventories and post journals from the late 1700s and early 1800s make it abundantly clear that cloth was an important commodity. In his journal for 1794, Jean-Baptiste Trudeau wrote that the Yanktons considered blue cloth symbolic of "the clear road" (Trudeau, 1914:423). Native American tradition confirms these early references. In one Sioux wintercount the appellation for the year 1792-1793 was "Woman in A Red Dress Killed". The accompanying mnemonic pictograph shows an Indian woman in a square-cut scarlet tradecloth dress (Lessard, 1980:2).

Sioux dresses were often made from two large rectangular pieces of cloth oriented vertically.

Although the existence of tradecloth dresses can be dated back to at least the turn of the 19th century, what remains unclear is the extent of their use and popularity. Because there are comparatively few early 1800s references to such tradecloth dresses, it is difficult to speculate in terms of a percentage of cloth to buckskin. However, evidence does suggest that by the 1840s, tradecloth dresses were becoming more common. The 1843 journal of Theodore Talbot specifically mentions Oglala women wearing both buckskin dresses and ones of tradecloth (Talbot, 1931:49). In the mid-1850s, German artist Frederick Richard Petri painted a watercolor portrait of a young Southern Plains woman wearing a square-cut blue cloth dress with red sleeves and side gussets (Petri, 1978:48). Cloth dresses became popular fashion with Native women throughout the Great Plains.

The saved-list tradecloth used in early period dresses was a woolen fabric often referred to by traders as "stroud", because of its principal place of manufacture when it was first introduced. Some of this cloth was rather coarse, but other (especially early) cloth was as fine as rainbow selvedge broadcloth. See the sidebar on page 21 for more detailed information. In many cases the white selvedges were incorporated as decoration "at the ends of the sleeves and along the lower edge" of early dresses (Holm, 1958:47). The North American Indian trade was a significant "market" for stroud cloth, at least during the 18th and 19th centuries, and the most obtainable - and affordable - colors were dark blue, and red, which was

Figure 3.49 Slow Bull's wife, Sioux, wearing a "saved list" tradecloth dress decorated with dentalium shells, which are also used for the earrings. A simple belt, bone hairpipe breastplate and hairpipe and bead necklace worn "bandolier" style complete the outfit. Courtesy of Libray of Congress, Photo No. LCUSZ62-50160.

generally referred to as scarlet. Dark blue (indigo) was the predominant color (Koch, 1977:134), with green and yellow available as well. Green was very popular among the Crow for elk-tooth dresses, and more so among the Plateau people, while yellow was in demand among the Sioux and Cheyenne for binding leggings and blankets.

Because cloth in general did not lend itself to traditional clothing patterns, which followed the irregular contours of animal hides, plains women redesigned garments in rectangular shapes (Conn, 1982:143). Sioux dresses were often made from two large rectangular pieces of cloth oriented vertically. These pieces became front and back when sewn together along what would become the neck-to-shoulder seams. Sometimes, however, the entire yoke with squared sleeves is one piece. "The neck is cut round (actually it is more often oval), with an opening down the back, closed by ties" (Holm, 1958:47). Sleeves were made by adding two additional squares or rectangles of fabric centered on the neck-to-shoulder seam and sewn to the bodice pieces. The sleeves of Sioux tradecloth dresses have been called "wings" because the bottom edges were not sewn together as in true sleeves and therefore hung independent of the wearer's lower arms (Holm, 1958: 47). To add fullness to the skirt area of the dress, Sioux women also sewed a tall triangular gusset into each of the two side seams. The gussets were purposely cut longer than the seams so that when they were sewn in place they hung down below the hemline of the dress (Lessard, 1980:73). These drops or tabs were a vestige of the deer leg extensions that had been "retained for decorative effect on earlier, leather dresses (Conn, 1982:143). This basic Sioux cut is the same for the Arapaho and Cheyenne.

Elk teeth are probably the earliest ornaments used on the tradecloth dress.

Generally speaking, most historically-styled Sioux tradecloth dresses are decorated in a similar manner: adornment items are sewn onto the yoke and hem region in distinct rows. Although variations in the types of items and the manner they are laid out give each dress its own unique look, there seems to have been a limit to the kind of ornaments used by Sioux women during the 19th Century. Primary decorations were confined to elk teeth, which were usually carved bone imitations, money cowrie shells, dentalium shells, brass buttons, and later, small coins.

Elk teeth are probably the earliest ornaments used on the tradecloth dress. However, dentalia became another "typical decoration" on cloth dresses of the Western Sioux (Koch, 1977:136). Dentalia, "tiny marine shells, traveled hundreds of miles on inter-tribal trade routes" before finding their way into the hands of Sioux craftswomen (First Voices, 1984:28). Up until mid/late 19th. century, several Northwest Coast tribes harvested dentalia shells. After these shells were cleaned and strung, they were obtained in trade by Plateau peoples living east of the Cascade Range, who, when they traveled eastward to hunt bison, later traded the shells with various Northern Plains tribes (Brafford, 1992:57). The great sums of dentalia made available to, and used by the Sioux, Arapaho and Cheyenne toward the end of the 19th. (and early 20th.) century came from Europe through traders. On Sioux and Northern Arapaho dresses, dentalia were usually laid out on the tradecloth dress yoke in "concentric rings" (Koch, 1977:136), while the Cheyenne arranged dentalia in straight rows. Cowrie shells, elk teeth, buttons and coins were affixed to the yoke in gently arcing or straight rows (Paterek, 1994:140). "Among the Plains Indians, for a woman to own a dress whose top was completely covered

with dentalia or cowrie shells was a sign of wealth" (Brafford, 1992:57). It was also not unusual to see a row or two of the same decorative item paralleling the hemline of the dress.

Secondary decorations on tradecloth dresses include ribbon, beads, brass or silver-colored sequins, hawk bells, and metallic fringe. Ribbon, particularly red, was often "sewn on in bands around the bottom, the ends of the sleeves, around the neck opening, and sometimes around the shell covered area" (Holm, 1958:47). Beadwork is somewhat rare on old Sioux tradecloth dresses although beadwork in tandem with dentalia has been noted on occasion. Sequins are seen as subordinate decoration, particularly along the hemline and down the sleeve from neck to wrist. Occasionally, one will see hawk bells along the hem and at the base of added ribbon drops.

Figure 3.50 Sioux carved bone "Elk Tooth" dress on blue saved-list cloth, featuring ribbon trim and brass sequins. Note that cut ribbonwork such as this is quite unusual. Courtesy of Morning Star Gallery. Photo by Ginger Reddick.

Chapter 3: Central Plains Dresses

CONSTRUCTION

This construction section will walk you through the making of a basic Sioux style tradecloth dress representative of the late 19th century into the 20th century time period, with the characteristic, long triangular gusset in the side seams and squared, open, wing-like sleeves.

MATERIALS

The basic material you will need to construct a typical Sioux style tradecloth dress is woolen fabric. The more expensive choices are saved-list cloth for earlier period dresses or rainbow selvedge woolen broadcloth, which is more appropriate for the late 19th century or early 20th century. More moderately-priced choices include wool cloth without white selvedge edges, a good grade of solid colored wool, or a lightweight wool blanketing, which is least expensive, but isn't optimal if bulky. However, beginning seamstresses are always encouraged to try their hand in creating a garment of less expensive material first, such as muslin or calico. Then as they gain experience they can feel more confident about using that costly piece of high quality, reproduction tradecloth.

Fifty-four to sixty inches is the ideal width of wool fabric. The optimal color choices for a correct 19th century look are dark blue or scarlet. Sioux women actually favored (and still do) blue almost exclusively. Many craft companies currently offer wool cloth for sale in a veritable rainbow of color choices including orange, white, yellow and purple. If you desire a truly historic look to your dress then I suggest avoiding these more modern colors. Stick to navy blue.

The amount of fabric required for this project will vary according to the dress size of the intended wearer. About three yards of 60"

Figure 3.51 Close-up photo showing the distinctive characteristices of "Stroud" or "Saved-List" tradecloth. Courtesy of Benson Lanford Collection. Photo by Benson Lanford.

wide material will be needed to make a dress for the woman of medium build. Larger dress sizes will naturally require more fabric. If matching cloth leggings are desired, it will be necessary to purchase additional fabric for this as well. Remember, when buying fabric it is always best to err on the side of caution as to the amount of fabric needed in order to complete the project.

For the comfort of the wearer, Sioux dresses are often worn with a cloth "underdress", an excellent example of which is shown in Figure 2.25 on page 23. Wool dresses can also be made with a lining; however, making and using a separate underdress is quite practical because it can be laundered, and if carefully made, can also be worn by itself. In fact, such an underdress is a wonderful wardrobe-stretching option on those hot summer days. To make the underdress, just use the same directions for the basic dress, but shorten the hem by an inch or two so that when the two garments are worn together, the underdress is not blatantly noticeable underneath. Making the separate underdress requires the same amount of fabric as in making the tradecloth dress. The underdress could be made out of any historically viable soft fabric. This includes two-color cotton calico, muslin, or perhaps even ticking, with its classic red-white or blue-white stripe pattern.

- **Thread:** Cotton or linen; a spool the same or a contrasting color as the tradecloth fabric. If also making an underdress, purchase a spool of thread to match it, too.
- **Binding:** Military braid, known as "Fox Brand", in white, dark blue, red or yellow is very authentic and excellent for use as binding; however, the colors are better as they do not show dirt. Bias tape, strips of cotton cloth, or ribbon can be used as well. Purchase plenty, as it will be used for binding the hem, sleeve edges, and neck opening. Ribbon adornment is more common on historic Sioux tradecloth dresses, but was only minimally used on earlier dresses.
- **Tape Measure & Yard Stick:** to take measurements
- **Seamstress' Chalk:** to mark dimensions on fabric
- **Scissors:** dressmaker quality
- **Pins:** straight pins plus some medium-size safety pins
- **Needles:** An all-purpose sharp, plus a narrow tapestry needle with a long eye.
- **Sewing Machine:** You may complete this project using hand sewing, or by using a sewing machine. Many people find the hand sewing tedious, but if executed carefully it does give the finished garment a certain air of "age".

DECORATION

If you want to decorate your dress with bone elk teeth, money cowrie shells or dentalia, purchase these items when you assemble the dress materials. Shells will be least expensive; elk teeth more costly. Genuine elk teeth are extremely expensive and virtually were never used on dresses of the era, with carved bone teeth being used instead. A number of reproduction elk teeth styles that are excellent substitutes are available on the Indian craft market these days.

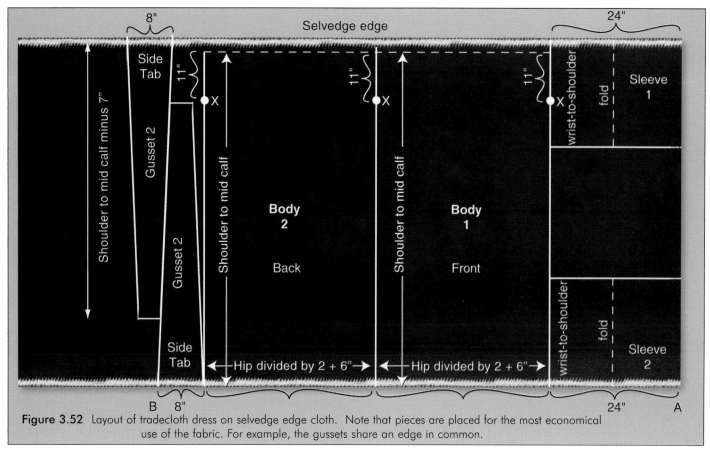

Figure 3.52 Layout of tradecloth dress on selvedge edge cloth. Note that pieces are placed for the most economical use of the fabric. For example, the gussets share an edge in common.

Decide how many rows of shells or teeth you want, keeping in mind that it is traditional to have the same number of rows on back as on front. Multiply this number by the average number of items (40) required per row. Thus, 6 rows x 40 = 240 teeth; however, more shells will be required than teeth, and these numbers will vary with different dress sizes. If you want additional rows of shells or teeth along the hemline, you must also add on another 40 or so per row. Special Note: You can save time and potential headaches if you purchase cowries and elk teeth with pre-drilled holes. To attach these to your dress, you will need artificial sinew, or very thin buckskin lacing, if you are patient enough to cut it.

MEASUREMENTS

To lay out the Sioux-style trade cloth dress, you will need to take three measurements; hip and bust, neck to mid-calf, and arm. Record all measurements and be accurate as they allow for a full fit to the garment. Extra fullness in the finished dress will be gathered in by the wearer's belt.

First, measure hips and divide by two, then add six inches to your hips or bust measurement, whichever is larger. Record this number.

Second, measure the distance from the top of your shoulder to your middle calf. This measurement, plus approximately 1" for shoulder seams determines the overall length of the finished garment. Modesty and historical precedent determined that Sioux trade cloth dresses should fall to below mid-calf length.

Third, measure from the outer point of your shoulder, down your arm to just over the wrist. This is the length-of-sleeve measurement.

FABRIC LAYOUT & CUTTING

Layout your selvedge trade cloth on a large flat surface, with the correct "nap" or texture facing upward and the selvedge stripes oriented horizontally in front of you. Remember that as you mark, cut and sew the cloth, you must keep the correct texture of the fabric facing the correct direction. If you think you might have difficulty identifying the external texture of the fabric as you proceed, mark it somehow in a consistent manner, such as with a safety pin, a pinned-on post-it note, etc. On all pieces, if your fabric lacks a selvedge band, mark the edges/sides noted in the instructions as being along the selvedge, with safety pins or some other clear symbol.

The Sioux tradecloth dress is made up of six pieces: a pair each of three different parts; rectangular body, rectangular sleeve, and long triangular gusset. Visualize these pieces as laid out in Figure 3.52. Note: the distance between A and B reveals the minimum length of fabric required for completion of this project. If you do your measurement math ahead of time, you can better gauge how much fabric to purchase for the dress. Frequently, the width of the cloth on the bolt was appropriate to supply the body of the dress so that the undyed selvedges of one end meet at the shoulders.

Mark out a sleeve piece with the following dimensions: your length-of-sleeve measurement x 24". The 24" length should lie along a selvedge edge. Cut out the sleeve piece. Using this sleeve as your pattern, mark and cut out a second identical sleeve piece of the same dimensions, again with the selvedge along the 24" side of the rectangle, as shown in Figure 3.52. Fold each sleeve along the line shown in Figure 3.52, and clearly mark the fold point on the selvedge edge with a pin, fabric chalk mark, etc.

Mark out a "body" piece with a width of: your hip-or-bust measurement plus six inches, and length of: your top-of-shoulder to lower calf measurement. Place the narrow side along the selvedge edge, then cut out the body piece. Using this body piece as your pattern, mark and cut out a second identical body piece. Place these body pieces as shown in Figure 3.52 and measure down from the top exactly eleven inches. Mark this

"Point X" on each side of both body pieces. You will have marked a total of four points.

Mark out a long isosceles triangle-shaped side gusset piece with a square point, as shown in Figure 3.52. The dimensions of this triangle should be as follows: 8" base and 4" top, with two sides tapering to the length of your shoulder-to-mid-calf measurement *minus seven inches*. Place the eight-inch base along the selvedge edge. Cut out the gusset. Using this gusset as your pattern, mark and cut out a second identical triangular gusset.

If you are using plain wool cloth with no selvedge, you can now sew bias tape, ribbon, or cloth binding on all edges marked as selvedge in Figure 3.52. Sew carefully. At the corners the binding should be folded neatly and tightly sewn. First, crease the binding with an iron. A binding of contrasting color serves the same visual purpose as the white selvedge. It adds a touch of color contrast to the dress as well as helping to prevent fraying and stress-related rips. If you wish, you can also add a second (and even a third) row of contrasting color ribbon alongside or up to one inch from the first one. Red, green or goldenrod colors look especially nice and are commonly seen on existing examples of historic dress.

To prevent fraying and tearing during wear, it is recommended that you take the time to "bind" all cut edges of the wool cloth pieces using a zigzag stitch on a sewing machine. For added security, this edge can be turned under a quarter inch and tacked down using a running stitch.

ASSEMBLY

Lay/place the body and gusset pieces as shown in Figure 3.53, and sew them together inside out, along the long seams, leaving the eleven-inch sleeve openings unsewn. Always sew from the armpit point downward toward the hem. The tip of each triangular side gusset must be set in at the exact bottom of the corresponding eleven-inch sleeve opening. This ensures that the base of each gusset on the finished garment will extend downward about four inches below the hemline of the dress. These extensions of the gussets suggest the earlier form of skin dresses (i.e., the leg skin hanging at the sides). Do not turn the garment right side out yet.

Along the upper edge of the wool fabric, cut out a small circular or gentle oval opening for your neck, as shown in Figure 3.54. This opening should be just

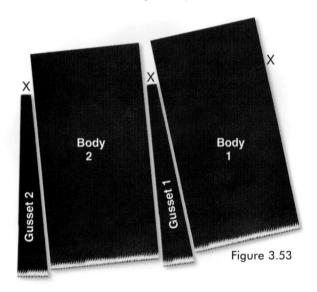

Figure 3.53

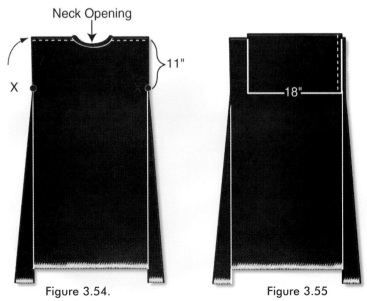

Figure 3.54.   Figure 3.55

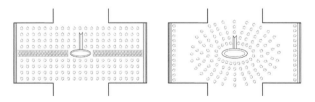

Figure 3.56 Typical layouts of elk tooth or cowrie shell decorations on dress yokes. Left: Cheyenne-Arapaho; Right: Sioux-Northern Arapaho.

large enough for your neck, plus an inch or so for comfort. It should also be just slightly lower in the front than the back. Sew along the upper edge of the body pieces, except for the neck opening. Turn the garment right-side-out and you now have a finished dress body, minus the sleeves. Both triangular panels should extend below the hemline at each side of the dress. All four sections of the hem will have an ornamented edge of either selvedge or bias/ribbon.

Cut one 4" slit in the center back of the neck opening, as in Figure 3.56. Check to be sure your head will fit comfortably through the opening. Using bias tape folded in half as a binding, stitch carefully around the entire neck opening, beginning and ending at the base of the slit. Take small tight uniform stitches and catch the bias tape above and beneath the wool with each stitch. Take a few stitches at the bottom end of the slit, to reinforce it, tie a solid knot, and cut off the excess thread and tape. This slit in the neck opening not only facilitates getting your head through the opening, but is the characteristic delineation indicating the back of the dress. Leave the ends of the binding

long enough for tie thongs, or add a thong at the top of each side of the slit. A piece of thin ribbon is preferable or a leather thong can be used.

Attach the sleeves one at a time, beginning by laying a sleeve wrong side up over the dress, as shown in Figure 3.55. The sleeve will fall approximately 1" below the crux of the arm pit, front and back. Pin the sleeve to the dress body and sew it in place carefully, going over the shoulder from front to back. Flip sleeve over, right-side-up. Repeat these steps for the second sleeve. Your basic garment is now complete. Note: Part or all of the underside of the sleeve is left open.

ATTACHING DECORATION

The Sioux-style tradecloth dress can be decorated with money cowrie shells or elk teeth. These traditional ornaments are attached to the yoke in concentric circles (a typical Sioux trait) or in straight rows (a Cheyenne-Arapaho stylistic element). See Figure 3.56. By laying the items out on top of the dress you can experiment with the overall appearance before making the arrangement permanent. For the best effect, the rows should be spaced a minimum of 1 ½" apart for cowries or 2" apart for elk teeth. Within the rows the items must be as evenly spaced as possible without overcrowding. If the shells or teeth are attached in straight rows, the items should be sewn down so that they are all vertically oriented. If concentric circles are used, the items should be laid out in a radiating pattern with the neck opening as center.

Regardless of whether you attach the shells or teeth individually or by row, each one should be secured to the fabric in three places by buckskin thongs, cotton cord, or simulated sinew (see Figure 3.58). The use of three tie-points is historic, not to mention essential in helping the shells or teeth to lie flat and straight. Double-check all knots. Keep the attachment lace as taut as possible without causing the fabric to bunch. On historic examples, it is not uncommon to see an extra row or two of shells or teeth attached near the edge of the wrist and along the bottom hemline (front and back). Sioux women were also fond of adding horizontal rows of brass sequins along the ends of the sleeves and bottom of the dress, and sometimes down the shoulder from neck to wrist. The decoration you choose should reflect historical tribal taste as well as your own preference.

Figure 3.57 Alice Lone Bear, Sioux, wearing a fine Stroud cloth dress decorated with elk teeth and ribbon. Her accessories include finger rings and bracelets, probably of brass or German silver, German silver concho belt and drop, and a long, breastplate of bone hairpipe. She is seated on a Navajo blanket, which is possibly a "prop" belonging to the photographer. Courtesy of Denver Public Library. Photo by F.A. Rinehart. Photo No. X-31516.

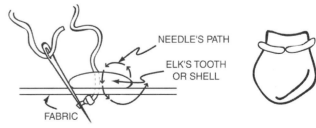

Figure 3.58 Method of attaching elk teeth, cowrie shells and dentalium shells on tradecloth or buckskin dress yokes.

Chapter 3: Central Plains Dresses

SIOUX Accessories

TRADECLOTH DRESS

Four wardrobe items are necessary accessories to the Sioux style tradecloth dress: moccasins, leggings, belt, and a wearing robe, shawl (often plaid), or blanket. By the latter half of the 1800's most of the moccasins being worn by Sioux women were of the hard sole type. There are a number of resources currently available to the interested crafter that can provide detailed instructions for the making of this moccasin type. Many of these resources also offer ideas for correct period adornment. Although workaday moccasins were usually either left undecorated or given minimal adornment, "dress up" pairs were elaborately embellished with quillwork or beadwork. Often the decoration on these moccasins matched exactly the decoration on the leggings (Holm 1958:47).

Women's leggings from this time period were of the simple tube variety, constructed from whatever material was on hand: buckskin, cowhide, tradecloth, etc. However, among the Sioux, Cheyenne and Arapaho, cloth leggings were quite rare. Sioux women's leggings were almost universally closed with ties; all were held up by the ubiquitous tie thong located just below the knee. Like moccasins, and depending upon use, leggings were either left plain or were ornamented elaborately in solid, lane stitch beading, usually with a white or light blue background (Ibid:47). Typically, the leggings featured a narrow vertical beaded strip with the opening toward the outside of the leg (Ibid:47). During the late 19th century, when the tradecloth dress was very fashionable with Sioux women, moccasins and leggings were often similarly beaded and sometimes matched one another, while the other accessories rarely matched.

Beaded bags such as strike-a-lite pouches, awl cases or hair-parter cases, a knife case or pouches for other articles were often worn suspended from the belt. Knife cases were also attached to the belt by means other than suspension; however, common methods included a slot in the sheath or a loop attached to the back through which the belt was slipped, or by simply thrusting the sheath through the belt. The extra effort a modern crafter puts forth in re-creating a full outfit has a big payoff. Complete outfits are not only spectacular, but are quite a testament to the crafter's skill.

A 2 to 3 inch wide belt of harness leather or thick rawhide is desirable. This belt was often decorated with large silver discs or brass tacks. Soft leather thong ties were often used and are historically appropriate for both belt types. Occasionally, buckles were used on the harness leather belts. An optional addition to the belt was a "drop", an extension that generally reached almost to the moccasin tops, and sometimes even dragged on the ground. For ease in use the pendant was often looped up and tucked into the belt on the opposite side of where it attaches to

the belt. The drop was constructed of the same material as the belt and was usually decorated in a similar style.

A serviceable set of tool pouches (also referred to as a "belt set") can be hung on the belt. Several of these are shown in Figures 3.45 and 3.47 on page 50. Arrange them in a manner that is aesthetic in appearance yet serviceable for you. In other

Figure 3.59. Mrs. Charlie Dunn, Sioux, wearing a cloth dress adorned with elk teeth. Her accessories include dentalium earrings with matching hair ties, a fine hairpipe and brass bead breastplate, tack belt with long double tabs, wide brass bracelets and a plaid, wool shawl with fringe. Courtesy of the State Historical Society of North Dakota. Fiske photo No. 2405, ca. 1908.

words, wear things that you intend to use, and wear them in a way they can be used.

The outfit you are assembling is re-creating an historic moment in time. The women of the past were engaged in the daily activities of life, not in standing around hoping others would notice their crafting skills.

A fringed shawl or a wearing blanket with the classic beaded strip was the perfect compliment to the tradecloth dress. Wearing blankets can be easily researched by studying old photos and museum examples from the late 1800's. The wearing blanket was correctly worn with the beaded strip oriented horizontally around the wearer. A painted robe in a box-and-border or stripe motif was also an acceptable wrap option.

Late into the 19th century, when the tradecloth dress reached its popularity and stylistic zenith, hairpipe accessories were still somewhat uncommon for women. While a woman's hairpipe breastplate can add to the overall look of the outfit, it need not be terribly long to be effective. Keep in mind that hairpipes are heavy and the longer the breastplate, the more uncomfortable it is to wear for extended periods of time. Although a long hairpipe breastplate is a highly impractical (not to mention historically inappropriate) item for everyday use at a pre-1840's living history rendezvous, it is an impressive accessory in the dance arena at a powwow. An appropriate addition for an early period outfit would be a dentalium shell choker.

Figure 3.60 The Dunn Girls, Sioux, wearing Stroud cloth dresses with dentalium yokes, sequins elk teeth and hawk bells. Note concho belts with drags. Courtesy of the State Historical Society of North Dakota. Fiske photo No. 5332, ca. 1904.

Figure 3.61 Mrs. Jack Treetop, Sioux, wearing a dress of saved list cloth decorated with several thousand dentalium shells and brass bells. She also wears huge, double-strand dentalium earrings, a long, bone hairpipe breastplate and a brass tack belt. An under-dress of what is probably a cotton print fabric is peeking out at the bottom of her left sleeve. Courtesy of the State Historical Society of North Dakota. Fiske photo No. 1104, ca. 1908.

Chapter 3: Central Plains Dresses

Figure 3.62 Sioux Dentalium Shell Dress - Hundreds of dentalium shells are used to decorate the yoke of this fine Stroud cloth dress. Ribbon is used along the bottom edge and sleeve edges along with ribbon trim accented with cowrie shells. Additional dentalium shells form sunburst style designs on the skirt portion of the dress. While this dress is the Sioux type, the Arapaho also used this style and possibly the Northern Cheyenne as well. The Cheyenne also used a dress with straight rows of dentalia across the yoke, similar to the dress shown on page 92. This dress is cut A-line, tapering outward toward the bottom, thus accounting for the absence of the typical side gussets, which was not uncommon among the Sioux in dresses of smaller sizes. Note that the panel beaded tack belt is a Ft. Belknap/Plateau/Crow style piece, not Sioux. Courtesy of Morning Star Gallery. Photo by Ginger Reddick

A Snake (Shoshone) Indian Woman

Karl Bodmer watercolor, ca. 1833

Wife of the *engagé* Marcereau. This popular Plains and Plateau two-hide style dress is shown with intact tail at the top front. Decoration with blue and white pony beads is also very typical of this period. Courtesy of the Joslyn Art Museum, Omaha, NE #1896.49-305

Chapter 4:
ROCKY MOUNTAINS

Historically, numerous American Indian tribes lived in the northern and central regions of the Rocky Mountain West. Using modern systems of anthropological classification, these tribes are not usually grouped along with the nomadic hunters of the Great Plains, but are typically identified as Great Basin, and Intermontane and Plateau peoples. Technically, this means that they are outside the scope of this book. However, certain tribes living in the northern and central Rocky Mountain regions during the 19th Century did exhibit many of the cultural characteristics anthropologists consider to be "classic" Plains. Is this because tribes such as the Shoshoni, Ute, and Nez Perce were influenced by Plains peoples, or because Plains peoples were influenced by their neighbors to the west? Historians have laid out lengthy cases for either scenario, but regardless of the direction of the influence, the fact remains that in the 1800's, Shoshoni, Ute, Nez Perce and others shared many cultural traits with Great Plains peoples, including mode of dress and personal adornment. In addition, and very importantly, they continued the use of the old style, mountain sheep dresses much longer -- in fact, some are still in use today.

Possibly the largest factor in this similarity was inter-tribal trade, which significantly pre-dates Euro-American trading ventures on this continent. In a nutshell, tribes all across the West were interconnected via a complex trading network which served to move desired commodities from their sources to their consumers. Some tribes gained reputations as middlemen; particularly the Nez Perce, Shoshone, and the earthlodge tribes. In their territories were centers of commerce where goods came and went with great regularity. Along with material goods like foodstuff, horses and slaves, came cultural influences as well. Hence many of the similarities of dress and deportment between Great Plains peoples and their trading neighbors on the geographic periphery.

During the 19th century, clothing styles among many Shoshone and Nez Perce and, to a limited extent some Ute bands, were quite similar to those of Plains tribes such as the Crow, Northern Arapaho, and Western Sioux. Except for a few minor changes, women's dresses were structurally similar. It is in the decoration of these garments where most of the significant tribal preferences are seen. In this chapter, we will be considering the basic history and structural characteristics of Shoshone, Ute and Nez Perce women's garmenting from the first half of the 1800's. The construction section will walk you through the making of a simple Type-One Two-Hide dress, offering specific steps and suggestions for modifying the basic pattern to create a garment indicative of historic Shoshone, Ute, or Nez Perce style.

THE SHOSHONE: DRESS AND ACCESSORIES

During the first half of the 19th century, a significant number of Euro-American explorers, traders, missionaries, and soldiers encountered the nomadic Shoshone or Snake people as they crossed tribal lands. Many of the men associated with the Rocky Mountain fur trade had Shoshone wives, not the least of which was Sacajawea, wife of hunter/interpreter Touissant Charbonneau, who was made famous because of her assistance to the members of the Lewis & Clark Expedition of 1804-05. Large numbers of Shoshone Indians could often be found frequenting the annual summer fur trade rendezvous. In fact, the great rendezvous of 1837 was held right in the middle of Shoshone country (Brown, 1996:396).

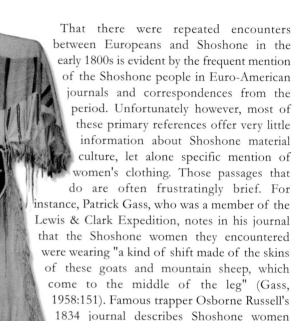

Figure 4.1 A classic Plateau-styled garment, the undulating line of the yoke (formed at the rear edge of the hides) was the basis for the curving layout of the beadwork. Beadwork is executed in a wide, loose lazy stitch. Note the retained tail, the addition of numerous beaded pendant thongs along the bottom of the large beadwork area, and the absence of beading on the lower portions of the dress. Courtesy of Morning Star Gallery. Photo by Ginger Reddick.

That there were repeated encounters between Europeans and Shoshone in the early 1800s is evident by the frequent mention of the Shoshone people in Euro-American journals and correspondences from the period. Unfortunately however, most of these primary references offer very little information about Shoshone material culture, let alone specific mention of women's clothing. Those passages that do are often frustratingly brief. For instance, Patrick Gass, who was a member of the Lewis & Clark Expedition, notes in his journal that the Shoshone women they encountered were wearing "a kind of shift made of the skins of these goats and mountain sheep, which come to the middle of the leg" (Gass, 1958:151). Famous trapper Osborne Russell's 1834 journal describes Shoshone women "neatly clothed in dressed deer and sheep skins of the best quality" (Russell, 1986:26). The ca. 1840 Letters and Sketches of Father Pierre DeSmet simply cite Shoshone women wearing leather dresses adorned with elk teeth (DeSmet, 1906:173). In his journal, Theodore Talbot, who was a member of Colonel Fremont's Expedition of 1843, mentions Shoshone women wearing long antelope skin dresses [literally "shirts"] with open sleeves and a neck hole just "large enough to admit the head" (Talbot, 1931:49).

Though they are brief, one thing most pre-1850 descriptions of Shoshone women's clothing do have in common is their reference to hide dresses. Various primary sources tell of dresses made from the hides of such animals as bighorn mountain sheep, deer, small elk, antelope, and mountain goat; however, it is quite possible that some of these observers were mistaken. While the Lewis & Clark journal seems to indicate that antelope were the primary game of Shoshone hunters,.it was most likely for a meat source, as most old Shoshone hide dresses in museum collections are made from mountain sheep skins, with the exception of one or two which are most probably made of elk.

The Lewis & Clark Expedition had many encounters with the nomadic Shoshone people. Thankfully, the various journals kept by members of the expedition contain several substantial references to Shoshone clothing.

Here is one description of women's dresses found in the official Expedition journal:

"Made from hides of the large deer Bighorn and the smallest elk...the Chemise is roomy and comes down below the middle of the leg; the upper part of this garment is formed much like the shirt of the men except the shoulder strap which is never used with the Chemise... [the sides] close as high as the sleeve. The sleeve underneath as low as the elbow is open, that part being left very full. The sides, tail and upper part of the sleeves are deeply fringed and sometimes ornamented in a similar manner with the shirts of the men, with the addition of little patches of red cloth about the tail edged around with beads. The breast is usually ornamented with various figures of party colours rought with the quills of the porcupine. It is on this part of the garment that they appear to exert their greatest ingenuity" (DeVoto, 1953:217).

Although this account is somewhat nebulous, certain parts of it do help to narrow down the style/design possibilities of the dress being described. The statement, "the upper part of the sleeves are deeply fringed," effectively rules out this being a slip-and-sleeve or a basically sleeveless side-seam style dress. That this description dates from 1805 also effectively rules out this being a classic three-hide garment as well. By the process of elimination, we are left with only one stylistic option which can "fit the bill": the two-hide.

What else can we deduce from the journal entry in question? "Come down below the middle of the leg," refers to a hemline at mid-calf or lower. Also, the dress in this description had deeply fringed side seams that extended from the wearer's armpit down to the hemline. The garment also had at least elbow-length sleeves. "Little patches of red cloth about the tail edged around with beads," notes a decorative feature common to many early dresses from the northern Plains and central Rocky Mountain regions. Though it is unclear from the journal description whether these cloth patches were actual fabric plugs that covered natural plunges in the hemline contour, or were simply ornaments basted onto the top of the hide, a study of historic examples reveals that both applications were common.

Euro-American artwork from the early 19th Century adds to the information derived from written descriptions, a much-needed visual glimpse at Shoshone women's clothing. Noted artist Alfred Jacob Miller was an eye witness to one of the annual fur trade rendezvous. He chronicled its goings-on on canvas. Several of Miller's painted images of this trading fair include Shoshone women. They wear loose-fitting hide dresses that appear to have extensive fringe along the sides and hemline.

Unfortunately, Miller's paintings that include Shoshone female subjects are panoramic in nature. In these instances, Miller was much more concerned with capturing a whole scene on canvas than being portrait-conscious by focusing on individuals. Consequently there is simply not enough detail from which to draw reliable conclusions about the specific clothing design and methods of ornamentation. One of the most significant early

19th century Euro-American painting that depicts Shoshone women is Karl Bodmer's striking portrait, "Snake Wife of Marcereau", which is reproduced in all it's magnificent color on page 61. Bodmer's subject is definitely wearing a two-hide style dress. The classic retained tail on the undulating yoke is clearly depicted. Several pairs of long decorative leather thongs hang down from it. A lane of what looks to be lane stitch beadwork in light blue and white beads, probably of pony bead size, extends down the top of each sleeve and across the upper central portion of the yoke near the neck opening. This young woman is wearing a dress representative of the early 1800's Shoshone style.

Accessories appropriate for the early 19th century Shoshone dress include moccasins, leggings, a soft leather belt or a narrow "panel" or tack belt for a later impression, and a hide robe perhaps painted in a simple geometric pattern such as the border-and-hourglass. Father DeSmet's writings mention Shoshone women's moccasins being made from deer skin and decorated with brightly colored quillwork. The journal of the Lewis & Clark Expedition notes that Shoshone moccasins of that time were "formed with one seam on the outer edge of the foot" (DeVoto, 1953:216). This statement indicates that these are the side-seam style that remained in popular use among the Shoshone until at least the mid-1800s. Forty-five years after Lewis & Clark, Theodore Talbot's journal still notes Shoshone use side-seam moccasins. In fact, the Shoshone and other Plateau peoples have never given up the side-seam moccasin, and at least two other major moccasin types were in use by all of them concurrently with the side-seam.

Shoshone women's knee-length leggings were held in place with a garter encircling the leg just below the knee. "Neither fringed nor ornamented...these leggings are made of the skins of the antelope" and the lower end of them were covered and confined by the moccasins (DeVoto, 1953:217). By the 1830's Shoshone women were also making cloth leggings. In 1834, J. K. Townsend and his compatriots gave pieces of scarlet cloth to the Shoshone Indians they encountered, which the women made into leggings, as Townsend's diary later notes (Townsend, 1905). A few years later, Father DeSmet mentions Shoshone women's leggings being made from doe skin, as well as from scarlet tradecloth (DeSmet, 1906:173).

THE UTE: DRESS AND ACCESSORIES

Historically, the geographic territory covered by the Ute in their rovings was quite vast, possibly because much of the land was desolate. Where resources are meager, basic subsistence requires the use of large tracts of land. Ute bands ranged widely with historic Ute "stomping grounds" extending outward in all directions from what would later become Eastern Utah and Western Colorado. Although the Ute are typically identified by anthropologists as Great Basin people, many bands had cultural characteristics in common with Plains nomads, including clothing style, and some bands should be considered central intermontane.

As with the Shoshone, the Ute were first encountered very early by the Spanish from New Mexico, and then later during the 1800's

Chapter 4: The Rocky Mountains

by Euro-American travelers in the west, including trappers, traders, explorers and missionaries. Unfortunately though, many of these encounters received little attention in primary journals. Only a small handful of written accounts mention clothing, and few give any specific details. For instance, in his diary, William H. Ashley, who had extensive involvement in Western fur trade and commerce, said that Ute women wore dresses made from the skins of mountain sheep, and robes from the hides of the bison. He went on to praise Ute women's clothing in general, noting that these clothing items were "superior" to those of "any band of Indians in my knowledge West of Council Bluffs" (Dale, 1918:81). Considering that Ashley quite literally had business interests all over the west, this is an interesting observation. But the diary entry like most from the period is woefully lacking in descriptive details which might offer clues as to the historic styles and adornment of Ute women's dresses.

Rather than relying on written material for information, we instead turn to the study of artifacts in museum collections. From examining extant dresses from The Chicago Field Museum, Denver Art Museum and The National Museum of the American Indian, with reliable provenance, we learn that Ute women's clothing from the first half of the 19th century is structurally similar to that of the nomadic Shoshone. Type-1 and Type-2 two-hide dresses are typical of the early 1800's. Most of these garments are made from animal hides identified as that of bighorn sheep and antelope. The dresses often have the retained tail on a gently undulating yoke, and a natural rather than straight-cut hemline. Occasionally the top portions of these garments are painted with a mustard yellow pigment. Additionally, many early Ute dresses have deep hemline plunges accented with fabric plugs – a trait which we usually associate with Upper Missouri clothing. Yes, there is clear evidence that garmenting and adornment styles were being adopted and shared between many western tribes.

After the middle 1800's, some Southern Ute women began making use of a narrow over cape similar in style to that worn by Jicarilla Apache women. This overcape or yoke, resembling the undulating sheep-tail form of the yoke on earlier two-hide dresses, was worn on the shoulders over the woman's dress proper, whether leather or cloth. The capelet sported wide beaded bands along the outer edge. Executed in lane stitch, these bands, were typically laid out in a horizontally-oriented, undulating bold stripe pattern created by alternating light and dark beadwork lanes, generally using only black and white colored beads. I would be remiss if I did not point out that stylistically, this use of horizontally-oriented, alternating light-dark-light-dark beaded lanes is strikingly similar to the bold beaded stripes commonly found on Blackfoot and other Plateau tribes' dresses, and to the alternating stripe patterns noted on some Cheyenne and Arapaho women's leggings.

Historically, women of the Ute tribe accessorized their dresses with snug-fitting leather moccasins and knee-length leggings, a belt and a robe. Though hide robes are the oldest traditional female wrap, according to one early 19th century source, Ute women were making use of blankets during this time too, and Ute men and

women also used Navajo blankets extensively. Carvalho noted that they were fond of red and blue blankets and often used them, "in the manner of a Roman toga" (Carvalho, 1973:20). Actually, this is somewhat misleading as, like others, the Ute were fond of the navajo "chief blankets", especially 1st and 2nd phase blankets, as well as classic, Navajo "serape" blanket styles.

After commercial harness leather became available to them, Ute women adopted the custom of wearing wide belts. Some of these belts were partially covered with tradecloth (scarlet was a favorite color) and beaded "panel" style. Robert Lindneux's famous portrait of Chipeta, wife of Ouray, illustrates this belt type. Other belts were garnished by extensive brass tackwork (Paterek, 1994:202) and extra wide, tacked belts with pendants were also worn by Earthlodge women, and even by some Sioux.

THE NEZ PERCE: DRESS AND ACCESSORIES

During the 19th century, and undoubtedly pre-dating this for considerable time, Nez Perce territory was the region stretching

Figure 4.2 As is typical of many other Intermontane dresses, this Ute dress is made of two large mountain sheep skins with the tails retained as front and back bodice ornaments. Traditional elements of Ute design include the three-forked cut of the bottom edge (created by the untrimmed shape of the deer's forelegs and neck), large zones of yellow paint across top and bottom, and patches of red and blue cloth at the throat and hem. Ca. 1880, leather, beads, cloth, paint. 50 inches long. Courtesy of Denver Art Museum. Photo No. 1985.51

from present day east-central Washington and Oregon eastward into Idaho. Nez Perce material culture was similar to that of other Basin and Plateau peoples. In fact according to their journals, when members of the Lewis & Clark Expedition first encountered the Nez Perce in 1805, they noticed many cultural similarities between the Nez Perce and the Shoshone, including their clothing styles. At this time, Nez Perce women were wearing simple unbelted ankle-length dresses of mountain sheep or bighorn hides. Clark called them "ibex" and "goat". (DeVoto, 1953:246). Their dresses were further described as sporting quilled and/or beaded decoration as well as small brass and shell ornaments. Although expedition journals do not verbally illustrate Nez Perce women's dresses in any degree of exacting detail, the fact that Clark said their dresses were similar in appearance to those they had seen Shoshone women wearing is significant. It testifies to the ubiquitous use of the early two-hide dress style.

One thing that primary written accounts do seem to be clear about with regard to historic Nez Perce dresses is the presence of beaded and quilled decoration. In his Narrative, John Townsend notes Nez Perce dresses as being "profusely ornamented with beads and porcupine quills" (Townsend, 1905:196). In the early 1830s, Warren A. Ferris wrote a general description of the garmenting of Rocky Mountain Indians in the Northwest, in which he described women's dresses as "long gowns of Bighorn hide decorated at neck and shoulders with all the beads they can procure." These dresses, Ferris continues, "are sometimes loaded with some eight or ten pounds of large cut glass beads (emphasis added) of various colors as well as other decorative trinkets and shells" (Ferris, 1940:291-292). This reference offers two significant insights into early 19th Century Native American culture: first, that lavish bead adornment on women's garments considerably pre-dates the Reservation Era; and second, that cut glass beads were in significant demand this early. These traits are well-represented by the beautiful dress collected by Spalding in the Nez Perce Museum, Spalding, Idaho, which is decorated with rows of three or four colors of large faceted beads.

By the middle of the 1800's, Nez Perce women were still wearing the two-skin dress style with the tail retained front and back. Well into the mid-to-late1800's, they favored the two-hide dress style, although by this time the yoke usually exhibited the downward dip in the center, front and back, without the actual retained tail. On "dress up" garments the yoke and the area of the dress bodice directly beneath the yoke, was heavily ornamented with beads. Typically, the beadwork on the yoke was executed in a somewhat loose, wide lane stitches, in bold, contrasting color, geometric patterns leaning heavily on various shades of medium blue as a primary color base. Beads strung on thongs often hung down from beneath this beaded area, adding a pleasing ripple of color to the dress when worn on an active body. Leather fringes adorned the side seams, the bottom of the dress, and sometimes the edges of the yoke. Nez Perce dresses often had multiple rows of decorative thongs across the lower portion of the garment. The

dew claws were sometimes retained where present in the natural cut of the hides forming the dress (Paterek, 1994:228). These basic elements are still popular with Plateau women even today. According to several primary sources, Nez Perce women were apparently beginning to incorporate cloth into their garment construction as early as the 1830s. In 1834, John K. Townsend wrote that they were wearing "dresses...of thin deer or antelope skin, with occasionally a bodice of some linen stuffs, purchased from the whites." Townsend observed one young woman "dressed in a great super abundance of finery, glittering with rings and beads, and flaunting in broad bands of scarlet cloth" (Townsend, 1905:272).

Nez Perce cloth dresses would fall under Holm's "northwest" stylistic classification independent from the "Crow" and "Sioux"styles. Made from tradecloth, corduroy, felt, velvet and similar fabrics, the Nez Perce style cloth dress, which includes a dozen or so other tribes in the region, usually has a "seam along the upper edge, where the skirt joins the yoke," and the sleeves, which are somewhat short, are commonly pieced onto the bodice. According to Holm,"of the three styles, this one follows most nearly the form of the decorated skin dress" (Holm, 1958:44-45). This is emphasized by the beadwork on the upper dress bodice, which is laid out to resemble that of earlier leather dresses, yoke and all.

Figure 4.3 Plateau (Nez Perce?) Dress, ca. 1880. Two skin dress of mountain sheep hide with tail. Yoke is decoated with red, green black, white and pumpkin pony beads. 48" wide x 54" long. Courtesy of Morning Star Gallery. Photo No. 20944.

Chapter 4: The Rocky Mountains

Like their Flathead and Crow neighbors, Nez Perce women wore soft hide moccasins and knee-length leggings, both ornamented with porcupine quillwork or beadwork (Ferris, 1940:292). For at least the Nez Perce, side-seam moccasins were undecorated. Leggings, however, were beaded, usually in floral designs.

Nez Perce women also wore leather belts and bison and elk skin robes decorated with beads. The Lewis & Clark journal specifically mentions that Nez Perce women braided their hair in two braids, just like the men (Biddle, 1962:171).

John Townsend's Journal notes the Nez Perce women's fondness for wearing multiple bead necklaces. They were fond of many kinds of decorations, in particular white beads, brass ornaments and vermilion (Ferris, 1940:292). However, according to Lewis & Clark, for Nez Perce women, the value of blue beads "may be justly compared to gold and silver among civilized nations" (DeVoto, 1953:385). The admiration and status of blue beads is common among many central and northern Plains and Rocky Mountain tribes. It has been said that because a true blue was one of the most difficult colors to achieve with natural pigments, blue beads were considered exceptionally valuable and were accorded a high trade value. With the exception of the sky, a few birds and some flowers, blue is an elusive color in nature, thus contributing to the treasured value of blue beads (and cloth). In fact, a study of trading post records reveal that at many posts blue beads were traded at a rate of nearly three-to-one over beads of other colors. The next two most popular colors were white and black, although these were frequently the only colors available.

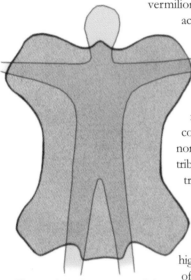

Figure 4.4 Orientation of the hides for the front and back of a two-hide dress.

This construction section will walk you through the steps needed to create a basic two-hide style dress representative of those worn by women of the Rocky Mountain tribes during the early-to-middle-1800s. The section will also include suggestions for structural and decorative variations that can be implemented to give the finished garment a more specifically Shoshone, Ute or Nez Perce look. Because we will be constructing a Type-1 garment with the actual turned down yoke, brain-tanned hides are strongly recommended. To achieve an optimal finished look to the garment, you should acquire hides which have the correct "from-the-animal" look. If possible the hides should also have the retained tail of the animal still in place, and a tiny edging of the hair retained along the entire butt end. If it is feasible and you are able to do so, you might consider tanning the hides for this project yourself in order to meet these expectations.

Commercially tanned hides can be used in this project if necessary, but they must meet very rigid requirements. The hides must have the appropriate from-the-animal shape (see Figure 4.4), and they must have as uniform a texture and color front-to-back as possible. Often, the only way to achieve this uniformity of texture is to physically alter the appearance of the leather. This is done with some good old fashioned elbow grease and a stretching/graining rope (see Figure 1.5, page 7). The slick side of the hides must be worked around this rope until the slick texture is sufficiently muted. So why is having the hides of uniform front/back texture important? In orienting the leather "smooth side out" for the dress body, you must turn the top part of the butt end of the hides downward to form the yoke - revealing the reverse side of the hide If it is of the to-be-avoided "slick" texture this will effectively ruin the believable old look you are wanting to achieve in the finished garment. Again, for best results with this project, brain-tanned hides are recommended.

MATERIALS

Creating the early Rocky Mountain two-hide dress for the woman of average build requires the following materials:

- **Leather** - Two large hides of appropriate shape. Each hide must have at least 16 to 18 square feet of good useable leather. Use the size comparison in Figure 4.4 as an approximate guide. Select hides that are especially generous in overall length (from neck end to butt end). Brain-tanned bighorn or elk hides are recommended.
- **Tails** - If your hides do not have the retained tails of the animal in place, purchase two small elk, bighorn, or deer tails which can be basted to the dress yoke to simulate it.
- **Scissors** - good sharp shears that can cut leather without giving you blisters.
- **Seamstress' chalk**
- **Straight Pins** - strong over-sized pins are recommended.
- **Medium size glovers needle** (or an awl and regular needle)
- **Sinew** - artificial sinew split down into four strands (or you can opt to use genuine sinew if desired)
- **Wool Tradecloth** - One piece (scarlet or blue) 28 inches by 1 inch, for the neck binding. If you choose a hemline contour that calls for "plugs", you will also need four pieces of tradecloth, each about eight inches square. These pieces should be the same color as the binding.
- **Workspace** - a well lit flat surface.

MEASUREMENTS & LAY-OUT

You will need the following measurements (in inches) of the person who will be wearing the finished garment:

    A. Back of neck to lower-calf
    B. Shoulder to four inches below armpit
    C. Body circumference at Bust (divide in half, & add 6 inches)
    D. Body circumference at Waist (divide in half, & add 6 inches)
    E. Body circumference at Hips (divide in half, & add 6 inches)

On a large flat work surface, lay out the two hides for the dress as shown in Figure 4.5, with the hairside surface of the leather facing up (if tails are in place they are up). If you are using commercially tanned hides, turn the "slick" side upward for now. From the center of the base of the tail, measure down four inches and mark this spot on both hides with a straight pin. Position the yardstick against this pinpoint and with the seamstress' chalk draw Line I (see Figure 4.5) horizontally across both hides. This will become your "fold" line later. For now it will be the benchmark for correctly orienting the lay-out of the other measurements on the leather. Repeat this process on the second hide.

Mark off the space for the neck opening of the dress by using the above pinpoint as "center". Measure outward along Line I four-and-a-half inches to the left and mark this Point X with a pin; then four-and-a-half inches to the right and mark this Point W with a pin. Repeat this process on the other hide.

Be sure that the length vertically down each hide from Line I to the bottom is at least the length of Measurement A (which you can measure and mark with another straight pin - this is Point Z). If there is too little hide to do this, the hemline of the finished dress will be too short to be historically viable and you should immediately search for a different hide with which to do this project. If there is excess hide, more than an inch or two beyond Point Z to the edge, you can either look for a different hide or you can wait until the hemline is laid out in a later step, to trim off the excess. Using the correct size hide is very important for this project. Optimally old style two-hide dresses should fit the wearer with plenty of room to spare and have a modest mid-calf hem length. Remember: historic two-hide garments facilitated freedom of movement for an active lifestyle.

Using Measurements B, C, D and E, mark off the dimensions shown in Figure 4.5, placing straight pins at the appropriate points. Use the seamstress' chalk to draw visual guides only. Repeat on second hide.

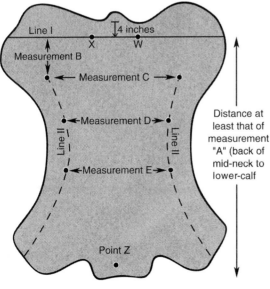

Figure 4.5

THE DRESS BOTTOM

To achieve pleasing continuity in the finished garment, the shape and contours of the lower edge of the dress should be nearly identical in appearance front and back. This means that in all likelihood you will need to do some carefully controlled "sculpting" of the bottom edge of the hides. Look at the shapes of the dress bottoms illustrated in Figure 4.7. These give you an idea of the overall effect you should strive to duplicate. If the bottom edges of both of the hides your are working exhibit this form already and do so at the correct length, you need to do nothing else to the hemline/bottom edge at this point. If however, they do not, now is the time to do some trimming. Begin by using the seamstress' chalk and the yardstick to measure and mark the bottom of one hide with the shape and contours that you desire. Because you are using chalk, you can feel free to experiment until you get the line "just right". Important note: Leave extra leather beyond this line wherever the hem contour you have chosen to duplicate calls for fringe. The extra leather you leave is what you will eventually cut into fringes.

When you are satisfied with the shape you have chosen and marked, use the scissors to cut or "sculpt" the bottom of the hide to this shape. Rather than cutting upward at the sides, simply continue

Figure 4.6 Plateau Dress, ca. late 1800s. This Intermontane dress is made of two large mountain sheep skins, featuring a heavily beaded yoke with other decorations of fringe, thimbles and shells. Note the undulating top border on the yoke and the typical, fringed bottom edge of the dress. Denver Art Museum Collection: The L.D. and Ruth Box Collection, Denver Art Museum 2002, Photo No. 1985.48.

Chapter 4: The Rocky Mountains

cutting the hemline curve in the direction it is already going, clear to the edge of the hide. If there is a dangling excess, don't worry. It will be dealt with later. For now, all you are doing is creating the actual line of the hem of the dress. When you are satisfied with one hide, lay it atop the other, matching Points Z, and using the hide already cut out as a template for doing the same with the second hide.

Lay the two hides out separately again, tails or "slick" side up as before. If the hem shape you chose calls for fringe, now is the time to cut into fringe the excess leather you left for this purpose. If the hem shape you chose requires the addition of wool tradecloth plugs, now is the time to create them and sew them in place. Figure 4.9 on the next page provides examples and directions for this. When finished, trim and fringe any dangling excess leather at the sides of the hem, as shown.

SEWING
Turn and stack the hides one on the other with the chalk lines and markings you made facing inside toward each other. Center

the hides with each other while carefully aligning the side seam lines (Lines II) you drew. You will need to look "in" between the hides by lifting and peeking as you go. Pin the two hides together along these seams. Be generous with the pins because they will be your guide for the next step, which is to sew the side seams.

Use a glover's needle or a regular needle and punch holes with a small awl and sinew. Begin at one armpit point and sew downward along the side seam/pin line you created. Use a very tiny running stitch. Keep the stitches small and tight and be sure that as you sew you are going down and up through both hides. Because the side seams are going to be on the outside, or visible when the garment is worn, the stitching must be extremely precise and uniform. Sew all the way down to within a few inches of the hem then make a "knot"

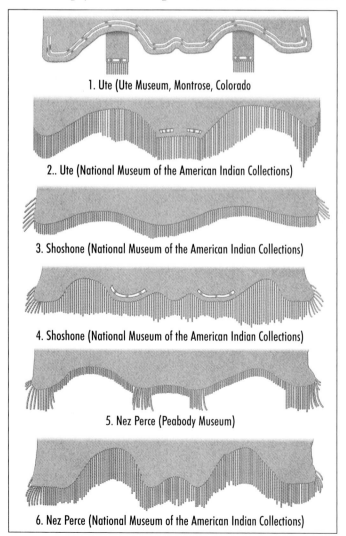

1. Ute (Ute Museum, Montrose, Colorado

2.. Ute (National Museum of the American Indian Collections)

3. Shoshone (National Museum of the American Indian Collections)

4. Shoshone (National Museum of the American Indian Collections)

5. Nez Perce (Peabody Museum)

6. Nez Perce (National Museum of the American Indian Collections)

Figure 4.7 Typical treatment of bottom edges of skirts.

Figure 4.8 Chipeta (Chepetta) and her husband, Ute Chief Ouray, visited Washington, D.C. in January of 1880. They were photographed extensively while there, with this possibly being one of the images taken. The yoke of her dress is in the classic style, with the tail area clearly visible. Note the simplicity of the beadwork merely accenting the natural shape of the hides, the added fabric squares along the hemline, and Chipeta's wearing of a sleeved cloth "underdress". The garment is accompanied by a wide belt of thick leather and utility pouches, all decorated with beadwork. Denver Public Library, Western History Collection X-11000056.

19th Century Plains Indian Dresses

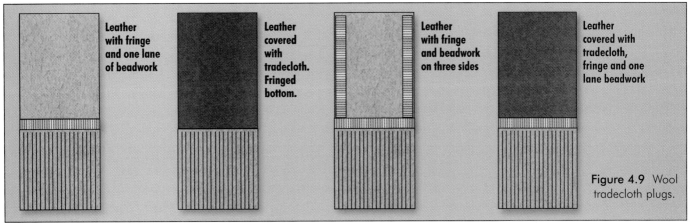

Leather with fringe and one lane of beadwork

Leather covered with tradecloth. Fringed bottom.

Leather with fringe and beadwork on three sides

Leather covered with tradecloth, fringe and one lane beadwork

Figure 4.9 Wool tradecloth plugs.

by taking a couple of backstitches and securely anchoring the sinew in itself. Repeat this process on the other side seam. To finish the body of the dress, use the scissors to carefully cut the excess leather left outside the seams into fringe. Leave a uniform half inch seam allowance, being careful not to accidentally sever the sewing.

THE YOKE
Referring to Figure 4.10, align Line I and Points W and X of both hides, keeping the dress/hides right side out. Pin both Point W's together. Pin both Point X's together. Carefully pin outward from these points along Line I all the way to the edge of the hides. As with the side seams, be generous with the pins because they will be your visual guide in the next step.

Anchor your thread or sinew securely at Point W, then sew outward to the edge of the hide. As with the side seams, use very small running stitches. Keep them tight, controlled, and uniform. To give your seam additional strength and durability, take one backstitch for every five forward stitches. At the end of the seam take several backstitches then anchor the sinew securely to itself. Repeat this process from Point X outward in the opposite direction. When these two shoulder seams are complete they will have defined the yoke "flaps".

To form the yoke, turn the flaps downward over the front and back of the dress. Use a narrow strip of wool tradecloth to bind the neck opening, as shown in Figure 4.11. Begin at the back of

the neck opening and progress all the way around, using a uniform large whipstitch. Keep the leather pinched tightly between the folded tradecloth, but take care not to bunch up the yoke as you sew. The yoke flaps should always lay straight down over the dress bodice. When the neck binding is all sewn in place, lay the dress flat and smooth down the yoke flaps.

Using a piece of extra leather, cut a dozen, thin leather thongs about ¹/8" wide and fifteen inches long. Use these to tack down the yoke flaps, positioning them as shown in Figure 4.12 with six on the front yoke and six on the back. If the hides you are working with do not have retained tails, now is the time to tack the "fake" ones carefully in place. Such pseudo-tails should be trimmed so they are not "bushy", and so that they blend in to the surrounding leather in as natural a manner as possible. The tacking stitches holding them in place should be secure but as inconspicuous as possible.

The basic Type-1 two-hide dress is now complete. Rubbing the yoke area front and back with yellow ochre can give the garment a distinctly Ute look. Beading the bodice section immediately beneath the bottom of the yoke edge, and adding a row of hanging bead strings beneath this will give the dress a Plateau feel. Choose accompanying accessories to reflect the same style tribal tailoring and the overall look of the outfit will be considerably enhanced.

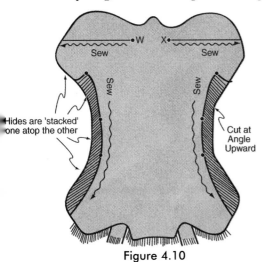

Figure 4.10

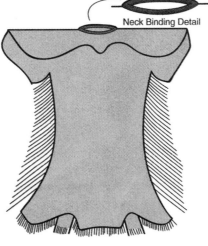

Figure 4.11

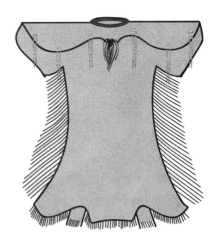

Figure 4.12

Chapter 4: The Rocky Mountains

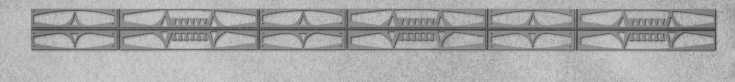

Figure 4.13 Nez Perce Dress, ca 1890. The heavily decorated yoke and shoulders are beaded in undulating rows, using four colors of seed beads (dark red, medium green, medium blue and light blue) and accentuating the typical sheep tail. The fringed decoration below the beadwork is made up of two colors of glass "basket" beads, a common trade item of the period. The lower portion of the dress, to include the side seams and bottom edge, is decorated almost exclusively with leather fringe. Denver Art Museum Collection: The L.D. and Ruth Bax Collection, No. 1985.42 © Denver Art Museum 2002

PLATEAU STYLE:
Trade Cloth Dress

In this construction section, you will be guided through the process of creating a mid-to-late 19th century Northwestern style cloth dress, as worn by women of the Nez Perce, Flathead, and other tribes of this Rocky Mountain region. Also referred to as a "wing dress" (see Shawley, 1974:95) this simple garment has short cape-like sleeves and triangular side gussets When made from woolen fabric, it was often worn over another dress of cotton or linen.

MATERIALS

The following materials are required to make a Northwest style tradecloth dress for the average size woman:

- **Cloth** - About five yards of 60 inch wide wool tradecloth (in blue or scarlet), calico, corduroy, velvet, ticking, or other appropriate fabric. If you opt for fabric other than tradecloth, do a bit of research on the subject so you can make a choice that will be truly representative of the 19th Century. A good place to start is "Printed Calicos For Indians" (Hanson 1988). Avoid obviously modern fabrics. Also keep in mind that different types of cloth require different sewing specifications (tension, type of needle and/or thread, etc.). If you are uncertain of these specifications, seek advice at the fabric store.

- **Thread** - Of matching color, and proper weight/type for the fabric selected.
- **Needle** - Whether sewing my machine or by hand, choose an appropriate needle for the fabric you have selected.
- **Straight Pins & Safety Pins** -- round-headed straight pins are easiest to handle.
- **Tape measure & Yard Stick**
- **Seamstress Chalk** - Do not use ink as it cannot be removed.
- **Scissors** - Save yourself a great deal of frustration by using good quality shears.
- **Binding** - Four to five yards of one inch wide ribbon or binding tape in a color that coordinates well with that of the dress fabric chosen. Avoid obviously "modern" colors.
- **Workspace** - well-lit, with a large flat surface.

MEASUREMENTS

Use the tape measure to take the following measurements of the person for whom the finished dress is intended:

A. Back of neck to lower-calf
B. Body circumference at bust; divide in half, then add 6 inches
C. Shoulder to four inches below armpit,multiplied by 2.
D. Measurement C, minus four inches.
E. Shoulder to elbow

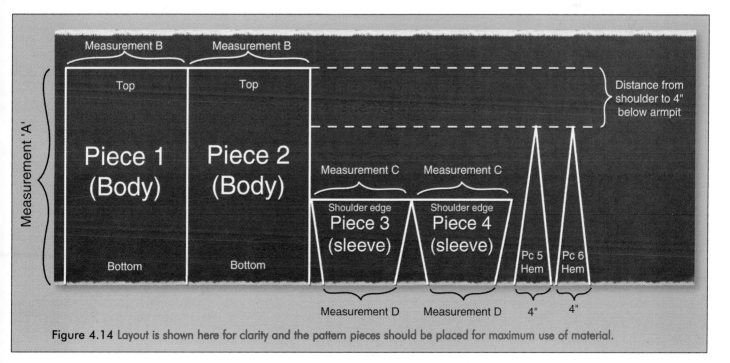

Figure 4.14 Layout is shown here for clarity and the pattern pieces should be placed for maximum use of material.

FABRIC LAYOUT & CUTTING

Orient the fabric as shown in Figure 4.14. If needed, note the position of the selvage. Using Measurements A through E, use seamstress chalk to carefully mark off the dimensions for Body Pieces 1 & 2, Sleeve Pieces 3 & 4, and Gusset Pieces 5 & 6. Cut these pieces out. If the fabric has no selvage, all outside edges should now be bound with the contrasting ribbon. These edges are marked in Figure 4.14. The binding serves to control fraying, and to offer a pleasing color contrast.

SHOULDER SEAM & NECK OPENING

Lay Body Pieces 1 & 2 on top of each other, with the "right" sides facing inward toward each other and the unfinished edges of the pieces oriented upward, as shown in Figure 4.15. With straight pins mark out a ten inch segment in the center of the top. This will be the head opening of the dress. Sew across the tops of Pieces 1 & 2, leaving a half inch seam allowance, and not sewing in the opening for the head. This joins Pieces 1 & 2 into the long dress Body Piece BP. (Figure 4.15)

While Piece BP is still folded, put the finishing touches on the neck opening. First, carefully "scoop" cut the opening (see Figure 4.16). Use ribbon to bind the neck opening. with small tight concealed stitches, not a wide visible "whip" stitch. Cut two leather thongs about 12 inches long and a quarter of an inch wide. Insert these through the neck area as shown. These are the tie thongs for securing the neck opening.

GUSSETS & SLEEVES

Open Piece BP and lay it out lengthwise, with the right side facing up. The triangular gussets, Pieces 5 & 6, which do not extend below the hemline proper, or selvedge edge, as the gussets on Sioux tradecloth dresses do, must be sewn into the sides of the dress body, and Sleeve Pieces 3 & 4 must be sewn onto the dress bodice area. Orient these four pieces as shown in Figure 4.17 and sew them into place. Be sure the "right" sides of the fabric are facing each other.

Fold the sides of Piece BP-1 (see Figure 4.18) up to meet each other, wrong side out. The sleeves will still be "inside" the folded Piece BP. Align the bottom of one gusset with the corresponding

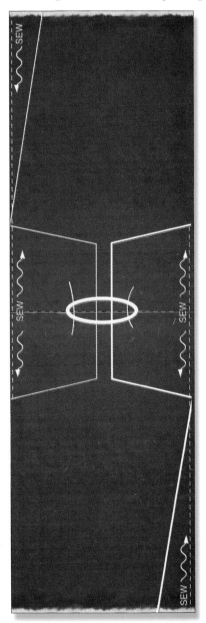

Figure 4.17

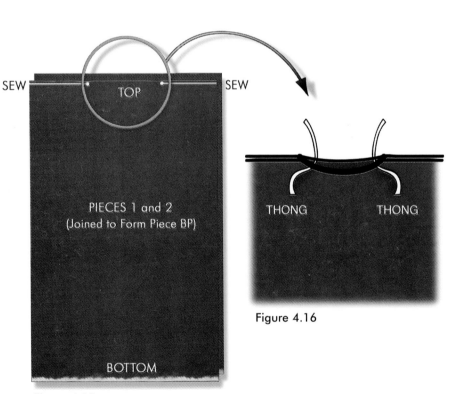

Figure 4.15

Figure 4.16

hemline/selvedge edge. Sew upward from the hemline to the point of the gusset, which comes to the point measured as four inches below the armpit. Do this for both side seam/gussets, as shown in Figure 4.19. Be careful to tie off the thread securely each time as these seams get a lot of wear and tear.

DECORATION

The basic northwestern style dress is now complete. Turn the garment right side out (see Figure 4.20). It is ready for decorating in appropriate tribal/historic manner. A few examples of historic Nez Perce decoration for this dress style are shown in Figure 4.21. By researching museum collections and exhibit catalogs, one can arrive at a decorative scheme that is distinctly Nez Perce in look. Remember to choose accompanying accessories that are in keeping with this same look.

Close-up of sleeve section.

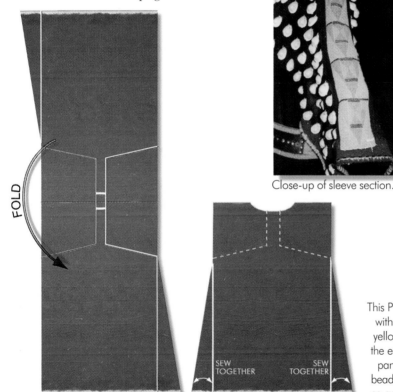

FOLD

Figure 4.18

SEW TOGETHER   SEW TOGETHER

Figure 4.19

Figure 4.20

This Plateau Tradecloth Dress from the late 1800s is beautifully decorated with wide strips of beadwork along both shoulders and sleeves, large yellow money cowrie shells, brass spots, sequins and cloth trim binding the edges of the sleeves and bottom. An interesting addition is the yoke panel of contrasting color red wool, outlined with a lane of light blue beadwork, and the red binding on the sleeves which has been "pinked" so as to resemble a saved-list, sawtooth type edging. Courtesy Morning Star Gallery, Santa Fe. Photo by Ginger Reddick.

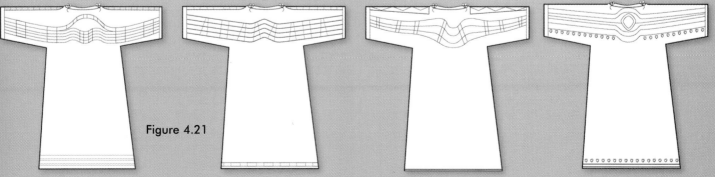

Figure 4.21

Chapter 4: The Rocky Mountains

Figure 4.22 Tail dress with the tail tab retained in the center of the yoke. Note the use of darker contrasting beadwork colors along the undulating edge of the yoke, which sets it apart visually. As with other dresses of this type, the lower bodice is unadorned except for numerous pendant thongs. Courtesy Morning Star Gallery, Santa Fe. Photo by Ginger Reddick.

19th Century Plains Indian Dresses

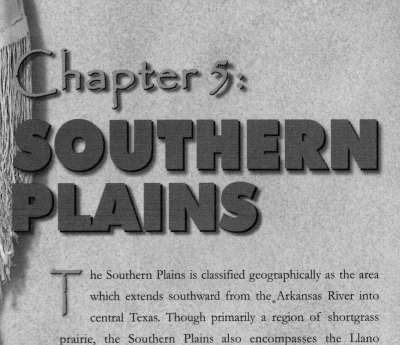

Chapter 5: SOUTHERN PLAINS

The Southern Plains is classified geographically as the area which extends southward from the Arkansas River into central Texas. Though primarily a region of shortgrass prairie, the Southern Plains also encompasses the Llano Estacado, the Red River and the Wichita Mountains. The Southern Plains generally gets less annual rainfall and has higher average daytime temperatures than the rest of the Great Plains. These climactic considerations affected the historic clothing of the Native Americans who inhabited this region and contributed to the development of distinct regional styles (Ewers 1979). This chapter will focus on the women's apparel of four Southern Plains tribes — Comanche, Southern Cheyenne, Southern Arapaho and Kiowa.

Figure 5.1 This very traditional dress shows the three-skin pattern the Comanche learned from the Plains Apache groups during the 17th century. The Comanches often preferred large areas of solid painting to beaded decoration on leather clothing. Late 1800's, leather paint, beads, cloth, ribbon, eagle feather. 53 inches long. Photo courtesy of Denver Art Museum, Photo No.1985.51

COMANCHE STYLE:
Yoke and Skirt

What sort of garments were Comanche women wearing in the first half of the 19th Century? One modern source offers this typical description: "The early garment for women was the knee-length skirt sewed up the sides with fringe along the seams and at the hemline. Over this was worn a poncho-like top made from one skin, with a narrow slit opening for the head, creating a high, straight neckline" (Paterek 1994:104). That Comanche women did indeed wear the skirt/top combination is borne out by several primary sources, most substantial of which are the written observations and physical collections of Jean Louis Berlandier, a Frenchman who traveled through Texas in 1830.

Berlandier's journal contains two of the earliest descriptions of historic Comanche women's clothing. The first description mentions only two items, "a shirt (*lit camisole*) without any ornamentation, and a skin fastened around their bodies to hide their nakedness." These, he said, were made of "tanned deerskins" (Berlandier 1969:51 - emphasis added). In a second description, Berlandier mentions three pieces of clothing. "They wear a sort of girdle, and skirt, and long stockings of tanned deerskin..." Berlandier 1969:115 - emphasis added). Though brief, Berlandier's comments are specific; the Comanche women he observed were wearing a top/skirt combination made up of two separate items. Furthermore, Berlandier also collected examples of Comanche clothing including a beautiful woman's deerskin yoke which survives today.

Ten years later, Victor Tixier, another Frenchman who toured on the Great Plains, also wrote of the Comanche. The information he recorded in his journal was related to him by trader/interpreter Edward Chouteau. Chouteau told Tixier that Comanche women "wear skirts and blouses of white skin, which are also decorated with paintings" (Tixier 1940:267). Like the Berlandier references, Tixier's description alludes to a 2-piece top/skirt combination. Was this combo the only type of clothing that Comanche women were wearing in the early 1800s? Were we to rely entirely on these two sources, we might conclude this. However, additional primary documents seem to suggest another female garmenting option — a dress.

Three New Mexico Chronicles contains an interesting collection of Spanish documents that date from the first half of the 19th century. One contains a passage which notes — in conjunction with comments about their modesty — that Comanche women were wearing long tunics with high neck and long sleeves (Carroll, 1942:129). (The chronicler also mentioned the excellent quality of the tanned hides used by Comanche women in constructing their garments.) In addition, Thomas Farnham's journal from 1839 cites that Comanche women were wearing "a long loose tunic which reaches from the chin to the ground, made of deer skin dressed very

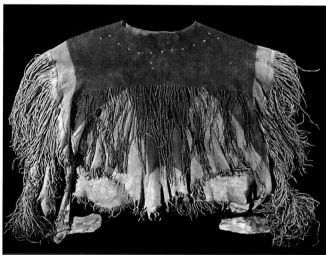

Figure 5.2. An early (1830) dress top or yoke attributed to the Comanche and collected by Berlandier. Courtesy of Smithsonian Institution, #81-4117.

neatly..." (Farnham, 1973:37). It is unclear exactly what form such "long tunics" took, but one thing does seem apparent: the 2-piece combo and the dress proper were in concurrent use by Comanche women during the first half of the 19th century. For the most part, by the late 1800s, Comanche women had abandoned the 2-piece ensemble for the dress proper.

What type of decoration did Comanche women employ on their garments? Thin fringe and pendant thongs are typical on early items. The Berlandier top retains the natural contours of the animal hide, including leg areas, and bears a painted field. Painting as a mode of decoration was also mentioned in period journals. Berlandier said Comanche garments were made of "specially prepared deerskin. . . trimmed with painted borders of their own design" (Berlandier, 1969:122). Farnham referred to dresses "painted with figures of different colors and significance" (Farnham, 1973:37). Colors used for this painting included reds, muted yellows and greens.

It has been asserted that "porcupine quillwork seems not to have been used by the Comanche" (Paterek, 1994:104). However, historical accounts seem to call this conclusion into question. For instance, according to one of the documents in **Three New Mexico Chronicles**, many Comanche women's dresses were decorated with embroidered "roses, carnations" and animal figures created from the dyed "quills of the porcupine instead of silk". The same chronicler adds: "These embroideries also indicate distinctions in rank" (Carroll, 1942:129). It is unknown whether this quillwork was Comanche produced or acquired from other tribes or in trade from the Spanish in Taos, New Mexico.

In historic times, extensive beadwork in large fields never became popular decoration on Comanche clothing. Beadwork was used sparingly and mostly as edging or "trim". Small beaded medallions were used occasionally. By the late 1800s, raw leather edges on garments were often ornamentally trimmed with pinking or scalloping. Dresses were occasionally decorated with horizontal rows of elk teeth or cowrie shells, and mescal beans were often strung on thongs to decorate the yoke and skirt.

THE YOKE

The skin yoke is the simplest garment to construct because there is very little cutting and stitching required. This is a garment suited to warm, muggy weather. Select a lightweight deerskin of medium size. If necessary, trim it to achieve the desired "from the animal" appearance. You can orient the hide horizontally (Figure 5.4) or vertically (Figure 5.5), depending on your personal preference and the amount of coverage you need. If your bust size is larger than 36, I personally do not recommend orienting the hide horizontally.

Fold the hide in the direction you prefer, and cut out an oval neck opening large enough to comfortably get your head in and out without panic. You can leave this opening "as is", or bind it all around with a small whip stitch (which helps prevent a droopy neckline resulting from wear). The yoke can be decorated with fringe, adornment thongs, and/or painting as solid areas rubbed with vermilion or yellow or green ochre were historically common.

A word regarding modesty: Remember that the yoke is an open garment. Depending on your activity, particularly bending over, it can be very revealing. Connecting the front of the yoke to the back by a tie thong or two beneath the armpit area is a step I strongly recommend. Although I believe strongly in preserving the historicity of the wearing of these garments, I also believe in discretion — especially when working with the general public.

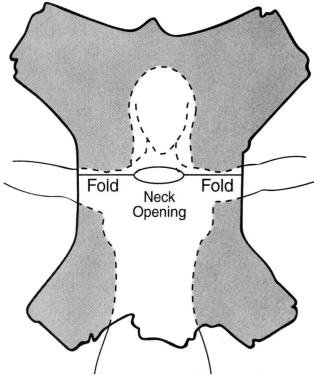

Figure 5.4 Most prevalent orientation of the cape of the dress.

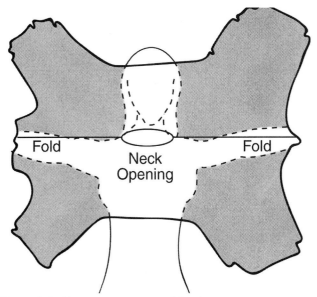

Figure 5.3 Alternate orientation of the dress cape.

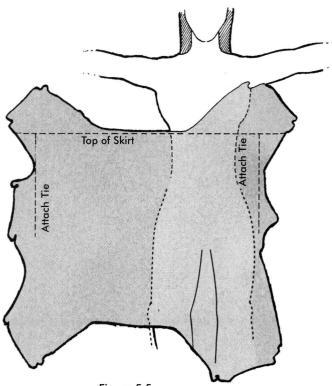

Figure 5.5

19th Century Plains Indian Dresses

THE SKIRT

There are basically two types of historic leather skirts: the 1-piece wraparound and the 2-panel. In the wraparound, the hide is oriented horizontally and wrapped around the wearer, producing an overlapping edge up one side and a fold on the other. The true wraparound has no side seam. Simple ties of leather were typically sewn onto the skirt. These were used to tie the skirt shut over one hip. Sometimes instead of trimming the top of the hide off horizontally, the extra leather was simply folded down in front and back, creating a small decorative flap.

The 2-panel skirt is created from two pieces of leather, sewn together. It can have a seam on one side with a wrapped overlap on the other, or two seams that close the skirt on both sides. The top of this type of skirt was almost always trimmed horizontally. Leather ties were added for wearing this skirt type wrap style. If the skirt was a sewn tube with two seams, small vertical slits were cut every few inches along the waistline through which was run a narrow leather belt. This arrangement could be tightened like a drawstring, and tied tightly. Old style leather skirts often retained the contours of the hide along the hemline. Decorative elements included fringing the hemline and/or adding a row or two of adornment thongs midway up the skirt.

Wearer's note: As with the leather yoke, it must be kept in mind that certain forms of this garment can be very revealing. I strongly suggest you use discretion when wearing a skirt wrap style, particularly if you will be wearing it in a public-oriented situation.

Figure 5.9 Detail of buckskin dress bottom showing placement of tin cones and method of attaching tabs and fringe.

Figure 5.10 Kiowa "Elk Tooth" Dress, ca. 1870, of the 3-skin, cape and skirt type construction. Courtesy of Maj. Gen. Michael C. Kostelnik, USAF (Ret.). Photo by Michael Kostelnik.

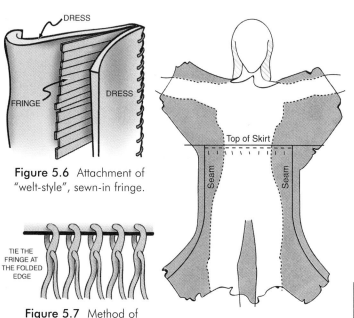

Figure 5.6 Attachment of "welt-style", sewn-in fringe.

Figure 5.7 Method of attachment of individual fringes.

Figure 5.8

COMANCHE Accessories

Southern Plains women usually combined their moccasins and leggings "to make one-piece boots with folded tops" (Conn, 1982:143). As early as the 1830s, Comanche women were wearing this 1-piece moccasin/legging combination. Berlandier described these as "stockings, which also serve as slippers" (Berlandier, 1969:122). Comanche women adorned their boots by fringing the folded top flaps and occasionally painting the leather green or yellow. By the mid-to-late 1800s, Comanche boots might also be adorned with a bit of beadwork and perhaps a row of silver buttons.

A lightweight tanned hide robe would be acceptable outerwear for the earliest 19th Century look. If a painted robe is desired, the border-and-hourglass design might be considered. Rather than a hide robe, a trade blanket might be the better choice for a mid-1800's outfit because by the 1840s, the well-dressed Comanche woman had replaced her buffalo robe with a blanket.

In his journal Tixier noted that, "almost all the red tribes which live near the borders of the United States wear the blankets that have been sold to them" (Tixier, 1940: 266-267). When choosing a blanket, be sure to select a historically correct style and color.

Several primary sources mention the fondness Comanche women had for jewelry. By very early in the 1800s, they were wearing traded bracelets and homemade bracelets made of traded materials such as copper and brass. Berlandier observed that, "bracelets of copper or silver and bead necklaces from which they hang silver ornaments are highly regarded..." (Berlandier, 1969:115-116). Bracelets and necklaces were often worn in multiple numbers.

Figure 5.11 Awl and whetstone cases, ca. 1870. Commercial leather, glass beads, tin cones. Heinz Brundl Collection, photo courtesy of Robert Wagner.

Figure 5.12 Comanche and Kiowa Ladies – Dressed in their traditional finery, these ladies are carrying fans and wearing otter hats (turbans), hightop moccasins and buckskin dresses with cloth "aprons". Although photographed in the early 1900's styles had changed little by this time. Seated from left are: Donald Big Cow, Mrs. Donald Big Cow, (Rachael Yellowfish), Cha Quaie (Rachael Yellowfish's grandmother), Ohne'veeta – Old Lady Whiskey Tom (Ada Bosin's mother), Maai-suta – Old Lady Mahsutky, Old Lady Fisher & granddaughter, Katahtah – (Ernest Tate's grandmother), Naa Kaah (or Ta tahkey), Old Lady Komanchee, Hu vu, Tha baenah, Wyiwuhneh – Cedar Tree Standing (Lee Motah's grandmother), Nuhsee – Gently moving (Owen Yackeyony's mother), and Oahthi – a Kiowa woman married to a Comanche. Identifications provided by Margaret Thomas & Sam Devinney. Photo by Sgt. Morris Swett, ca. 1926, courtesy of Denver Public Library, Western History Photos. No. X-32205.

Figure 5.13
Chi-wek-kiethe and Sister
This studio portrait is identified
as Chi-wek-kiethe and her
sister, Looking-For-Something-
Good (Cha-wa-ke). In 1982,
Evelyne Wahkinney Voelker
identified the woman seated
on the ground in this way:
"This is my grandma, Naa
Kaah. She was given to
Wah ah kinney. This was
my dad's parents. Her
name means, "For a short
time" or "Little while". I don't
know how she got her
name. She was very small,
stood only about 4' 7", she,
as I remember was also
slight in build...Wah ah
Kinney, "Comes Crying" was
almost 6 ft tall... a very
gentle man. He died at 60
years. Naa Kaah died near
her 100th birthday. They
lived on the bank of
Chandler Creek...
Comanche County, Okla,
15 mi north of Lawton in
the foothills of the Wichita
Mtns." These two Comanche
women had long, loose hair
and wore calico dresses,
bracelets, beaded strike-a-
light bag and awl case, and
high-top moccasins decorated
with pierced, German silver
brooches which were a
commercial trade item sold
by S. A. Frost & Co of New
York City. Frost carried several
styles of pierced brooches
for the Indian trade as well
as conchos and small buttons
commonly found on boots.
Note the cut ribbonwork
edging on the saved-list
cloth blanket, which could
possibly be from the influence
of the Delaware band living
near Anadarko. Her sister is
wearing a bold plaid wool
blanket. Photographed by
W. S. Soule sometime
between 1868 and 1874.
Photo courtesy of Denver
Public Library, Western
History Photos. No. X-32201

19th Century Plains Indian Dresses

THE THREE HIDE DRESS:
A Closer Look

The three-skin dress replaced the "trade cloth dress as the favored 'Indian costume' among Southern Plains Indian women who could afford it" (Ewers 1997:143). According to John Ewers, the three-skin dress "was a clothing style quite unlike that worn by Indian women of the northern plains at the time of first white contact or any other time of which we have any record" (Ibid:149). The style "involved a new concept of the use of buckskin in dress design as well as some elementary tailoring — the piecing and sewing together of three buckskins to form a true dress which covered the wearer from the shoulders to well below the calves of the legs" (Ibid:143-144). Ewers described the construction of this dress style: One skin, with a slit in the center for the head, covered the shoulders, upper arms, and breasts — as had the old poncho. But this skin was trimmed and sewn in a horizontal seam at the midriff to two other skins — one of which formed the front and the other the back of the middle and lower portions of the garment. This is also the basic structure of Sioux dresses with fully-beaded yokes and, even today, some Southern Plains dresses still retain this separate yoke. Advantage was taken of the broad natural extensions of the rear legs of the deerskins to provide needed fullness to the lower portion of this dress. The two lower deerskins were sewn or tied together at the sides" (Ibid:144).

Richard Conn (1955), has speculated that the three-skin dress evolved from separate skirt and poncho, concluding that the bodice (upper portion of the dress between the waist and shoulder) and skirt, when laced together, became the three-skin dress (Paterek 1994:104). John Ewers believed that the three-skin dress did not evolve from an earlier skin poncho/skirt combination, but was a style that "began to appear among these Indians at about the same time as did the tradecloth dress" (Ewers 1997:149).

Regardless of debate over its particular historic origin, the use of the three-skin dress is usually attributed historically to southern plains tribes such as the Kiowa, Comanche, Pawnee, Cheyenne, and Arapaho. Conn's Classification also cites Shoshoni use of this style, The Sioux used it as well, and even 20th Century Crow buckskin dresses are made in this style. One of the earliest illustrations of the Southern Plains three-hide dress is found in a watercolor portrait of Owl Woman (wife of trader William Bent, daughter of White Thunder, Keeper of the Cheyenne Medicine Arrows) painted by Lieutenant James Abert around 1845. According to Ewers, the oldest well-documented example of this dress is in the collection of the United States National Museum (#59,592). This particular dress was given to Commissioner F.V. Calver during the Fort Wise Treaty proceedings of February 1861, by Little Raven, chief of the Southern Arapaho (Ewers 1979:144).

By the 1890s the three-skin dress style had become a very popular style among women of most Southern Plains tribes. "By that time buckskin had become more difficult to obtain, and the possession of a well-made elaborately decorated skin dress had become something of a status symbol" (Op Cite:144-145).

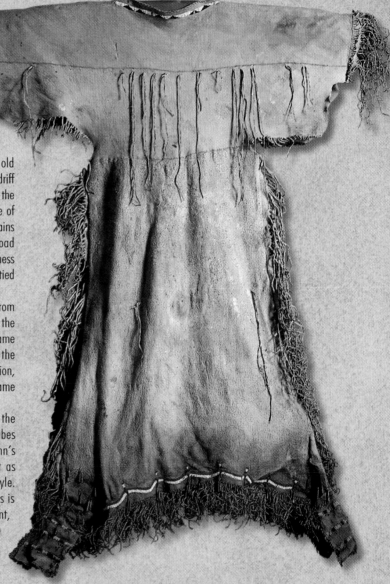

Figure 5.14 Comanche Three-Skin Dress
The simple elegance of Comanche workmanship is exemplified in this classic buckskin dress. The limited amount of beadwork is done in only five colors: white, red, dark blue, medium blue and yellow. This, along with the large painted area on the yoke, tin cones on the tabs and the finely cut fringe, are all typical Comanche decorations. Photo courtesy of Eleanor Tulman Hancock.

SOUTHERN CHEYENNE & ARAPAHO DRESSES

n *The Cheyenne Indians*, noted ethnologist George Grinnell quotes Cheyenne informants who said that the side-fold dress was typical women's wear in the early 1800s (Grinnell, 1923:56-57). The journals of the Lewis & Clark Expedition provide concrete evidence for this conclusion. Expedition members met a large contingent of Cheyenne at the upper Arikara villages along the Missouri River in 1806. The Cheyenne had come to trade and parlay with the Arikara. At the time of this encounter, the North/South separation of Cheyenne bands had yet to take place. The expedition journal entry for August 21, 1806, describes women's dresses "made of two equal pieces of hide, sewed from the bottom with arm holes, with a flap hanging nearly halfway down the body, both before and behind" (Biddle, 1962:215).

Very little is known about the Cheyenne method of decorating these early dresses, however, Lewis & Clark's journal mentions "beads, shells, and elk horns, probably elk teeth, which all Indians admire," as well as various "figures" burnt onto the garment "by means of a hot stick" (Op Cite: 215). (Editor's Note: Lignite, a soft coal-like substance which was ground and mixed with an adhesive such as hide glue for use as a liquid paint, could have been used. This was a common technique for decoration, producing a brown-black color.) The use of beads, shells and teeth comes as no surprise — but the reference to burned figures does. Because there are no known examples of side-fold dresses decorated in this technique, and as to my knowledge this is the only mention of it in primary journals, we are left to speculate about the nature of this statement. Perhaps the observer only assumed that these designs were produced by burning with a hot stick, as opposed to being applied with lignite-based paint, which would be the same color.

According to period sources, by the 1830s (if not earlier), Cheyenne women had largely abandoned the side-fold dress in

favor of the two-hide style. In 1832, George Catlin painted a portrait of the Cheyenne woman *Tis-see-woo-na-tis* (She Who Bathes Her Knees, wife of Wolf On The Hill). Although the painting does not show a yoke or bodice area at the shoulders of her dress, a tail is visible on the upper bodice. The garment is clearly of a two-hide style. It is tastefully adorned with a single lane of beadwork running horizontally along the shoulders — covering the seam? — and around the neckline, and incorporating a "sunburst" pattern on each shoulder, two small circles of quillwork at mid-breast, with pendant thongs and a single row of metal buttons along the neckline (Catlin, 1973:Vol. 2, 2). She also wears multiple bead necklaces and earrings.

Due in part to the exposure of Southern Cheyenne women to the garment styles and decorative mannerisms of their Southern Plains neighbors, particularly the Kiowa and Comanche, by the 1840s their dresses were beginning to look a bit different from those of their Northern counterparts. In his 1842 journal, Lewis H. Garrard (1955:54) offers a description of the dresses of Cheyenne women whose villages were in the vicinity of Bent's Fort. Garrard writes, "their dresses were made of buckskin, high at the neck" with "short sleeves, or rather none at all". These garments were knee length and fit loosely, "giving a relieved Diana look to the costume" (Ibid: 54). More significant however, is Garrard's next phrase wherein he refers to the edges of the hides as being scalloped and "worked with beads, and fringed" (Ibid:54). This is one of the earliest specific mentions of what is considered by most scholars to be a characteristic of classic Kiowa dresses. Is this an example of cultural borrowing? Perhaps.

The 1845 "Report" and artwork of Lieutenant J.W. Abert also illustrates the dress of Cheyenne women from the vicinity of Bent's Fort. Abert painted the portrait of *Mis-Stan-Star*, Cheyenne wife of trader William Bent. In his journal Abert noted that she had "put on her handsomest dress in order to sit for me". This

Figure 5.15 Classic three-skin Cheyenne dress, ca. 1880. Brain-tanned buckskin decorated with seed beads, tin cones, cowrie shells, paint and fringe. Note the distinctive "tabs" at bottom outer edges of the skirt. Photo courtesy of Morning Star Gallery.

(continued on page 84)

Figure 5.16 Southern Cheyenne or Southern Arapaho, girl's or woman's dress ca. 1870. Native-tanned hide, money cowrie shells, in light blue, white, navy blue and red glass beads, and yellow and green pigments. L: 45 in. W: 48 in. (with fringes). Heinz Bründl Collection, Photo courtesy of Robert Wagner.

19th Century Plains Indian Dresses

(continued from page 82)

dress, he writes, consisted of a "cape and undergarment...bordered with bands of beads" (Abert, 1846:4). Abert's portrait shows *Mis-Stan-Star* wearing what seems to be a garment of three-hide style. It is decorated with beaded strips in the common blue, black and white geometric patterns associated with pound beadwork of the period. The hem of the dress has a pigmented area enclosed in a gently scalloped lane of beadwork.

Lieutenant Abert also painted the portrait of another Cheyenne woman, *Am-er-tschee,* The Fast Walker, who was the daughter of *Nah-co-men-si,* second in rank to Yellow Wolf. "She is very rich", Abert writes of her, "possessing several complete suits of buckskin, all most tastefully ornamented" (Ibid:4). In the portrait *Am-er-tschee* wears a three-hide dress similar to *Mis-Stan-Star's.* She is also wearing a leather belt "studded with large flat gilt buttons" (Ibid:4).

Grinnell described the typical mid-1800's Cheyenne dress as a "smock or shirt made of the skins of deer, sheep, antelope, or elk." It reached from the neck to "halfway from knee to ankle. The sleeves were like a cape, open below, and hung down to the elbows" (Grinnell, 1923:Vol. 1, 224).

Grinnell also notes that the dresses of older women and the leggings of older men, "were usually made from buffalo cow skin, and for this purpose old skins that had served as the upper part of lodge coverings were often employed. Such skins had been thoroughly smoked, and were always very soft and durable" (Ibid:Vol. 1, 217).

By the early to mid-19th century, Cheyenne and Arapaho women were wearing three-skin dresses. Southern Cheyenne women developed a three-skin garment style with decorative characteristics that are now considered "classic" Southern Cheyenne and Southern Arapaho. These include squared off sleeves with long added (not self) fringe; coloration of the top hide of the dress with a mustard yellow pigment; retention of the hide from the animal legs as pendants hanging from underneath the sleeves or the addition of fake leg pendants if the hide did not have them to begin with; creation of a scalloped decorative area near the hemline, usually a narrow painted region enclosed in a narrow scalloped beaded border; a similarly pigmented narrow rectangular area underneath the neck opening front and back (this was also enclosed by a narrow beaded border); rectangular "tabs" hanging at the side of the dress, below the hem on both front and back skirt panels; and the horizontal orientation of added decorative elements.

The classic late-1800's Southern Cheyenne dress might sport a yoke covered with tightly spaced horizontal rows of cowrie shells or elk teeth, both of which were symbols of wealth and abundance. In fact, Grinnell wrote that among the Cheyenne "one hundred elk-teeth used to be worth a good horse" (Ibid:Vol. 1, 224). More often though, the classic Southern Cheyenne or Southern Arapaho dress would have three wide beaded strips, usually more than six lanes side-by-side. Two of these run horizontally across the center of the yoke, one on the front of the dress, and one on the back. The other strip went down the center line of the shoulder area, from the neck opening to the ends of the sleeves. Other beaded strips, a single lane wide, were also sewn across the middle of the skirt sections horizontally, oftentimes in conjunction with a row or two of long pendant thongs.

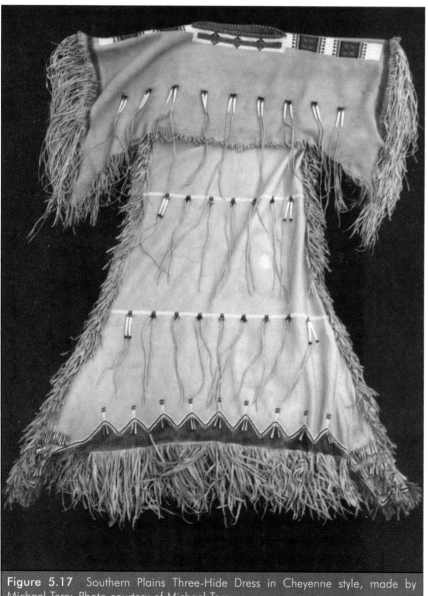

Figure 5.17 Southern Plains Three-Hide Dress in Cheyenne style, made by Michael Terry. Photo courtesy of Michael Terry.

CONSTRUCTION

The construction of a basic three-hide dress is, in many ways significantly simpler than the two-hide. The three-skin dress is made from three large complete deer hides; one for the upper bodice (yoke), the other two for the skirt area. The hides should each display the basic "from the animal" shape. To select the two hides required for the skirt panels of your garment, hold each hide up to you, orienting them vertically with the butt-end up. The two hides you choose for the skirt should be as wide as your body, plus four to six inches extra on each side. Although it may seem insignificant now, this extra edging will eventually become the fringe along the side seams of your garment. The optimal length for fringe is three to four inches.

If you are using commercially-tanned leather for this project you will need to take special care to keep the rough-side-out "texture", the same for each of the three sections of the dress. If you are purchasing hides in any color but white it is also important that their color matches as closely as possible. Should you wish to paint the yoke section of your dress, the hides you select should not be colored. The best time to paint the yoke section is before you sew this hide to the skirt panels.

MATERIALS

You will need the following materials in addition to the three hides:

1) **Tape Measure Yard Stick and Ruler**
2) **Seamstress Chalk** - or another non-permanent medium for marking on the leather.
3) **Scissors** - heavy duty
4) **Trade wool cloth** - A small 12" square is sufficient. (If you do not desire a contrasting color binding around the neck opening of your dress, you do not need this cloth.)
4) **Thread Medium** - I recommend artificial sinew, split to ¼" thickness.
5) **Needle and Sewing Awl** - The awl is for piercing the hole for the seams of your garment.
6) **Work Surface** - flat and well-lit.

MEASUREMENTS

1) **Waist** (plus 4-6")
2) **Hips** (plus 4-6")
3) **Armpit to middle of calf**
4) **Armpit to hips**
5) **Top of shoulder to middle of calf**
6) **Top of shoulder to armpit** (plus 2")

THE SKIRT PANELS

The two hides designated as skirt panels will be laid out and cut identically. If you wish, you can measure and cut out one panel first and then use it as a pattern for measuring and cutting the

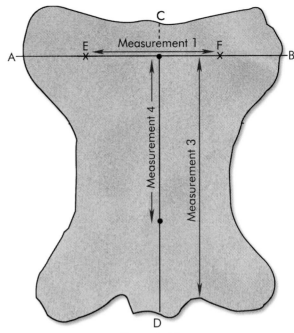

Figure 5.18

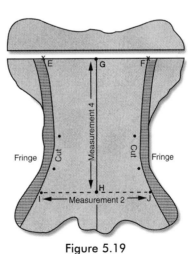

Figure 5.19

other. (Just remember to flip it upside down before tracing around it.) On the wrong side of one hide, use measurement #3 to determine the position of Line A-B. Draw this line in place.

Next, draw a vertical line right down the middle of the hide from the center of Line A-B to the bottom. This is Line C-D. Center Measurement # 1 to Line C-D and along Line A-B. Clearly mark each end of this measurement; shown as Points E and F on Figure 5.18. Cut the hide in half along Line A-B.

Using measurement #4, mark Line G-H, as shown in Figure 5.18. Using Line C-D, center measurement #2 along Line G-H. Mark one end of this as Point I, the other as Point J. Draw a gently curving line from Point F through Point J and downward to the end of the hide. Repeat for Point E through Point I. Cut along these two lines. Remove the two strips. These strips should be cut into fringe, leaving one continuous ¼" uncut edge (see Figure 5.18). You now have one complete skirt panel. You can flip this panel upside-down over onto the other hide (which is laying wrong side up) and use it as a guide for marking the other hide with the same dimensions. Cut out the two strips from this hide and fringe them as you did the others. When you are finished, you will have two compatible skirt panels and four large sections of fringe.

YOKE

The upper portion of this dress will be made from the third hide you have selected. It will be oriented horizontally, as shown in Figure 5.21. Begin with the wrong (slick) side of the hide up. Draw a line bisecting the middle of the hide in each direction. Label these Lines U-V and W-X, as in Figure 5.21. Using measurement #6 to determine how far from Line U-V to go, mark Lines y/z and y'/z' onto the hide. Center Measurement #1 onto Lines y/z and y'/z' and mark a point at each end. Designate these Points as Y,Z,Y',and Z', as per Figure 5.21. Draw a line straight out from each of these points to the edge of the hide. Cut out the small strips thus outlined (they are the small shaded areas on Figure 5.21). Keep the hide wrong side up.

The neck opening of the yoke section comes next. Determine how wide this opening should be to be able to get

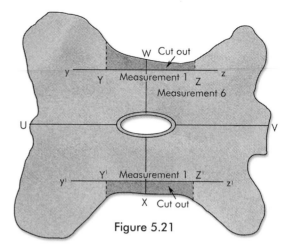

Figure 5.21

Figure 5.20 Ester Clark, Comanche – Daughter of Woom-ah-kony and Edward L. Clark. This studio portrait, taken between 1890 and 1910, shows Ester Clark wearing a fine Cheyenne buckskin dress, with a fringed, Pendleton type robe with a star and diamond banded pattern draped around her shoulders. Note her fully beaded Cheyenne moccasins and leggings, fringed tassels of a sash or belt, extra long bone hairpipe necklace, beaded headband, and what appears to be a fully beaded bag under her right hand. Photo courtesy of Denver Public Library, Western History Photos # X-32202

your head through comfortably (typically somewhere around 10-12"). Center the opening on Line U-V, as in Figure 5.21. For maximum comfort, the neck opening should be cut in the shape of a gentle oval. Southern Plains dresses were often painted with a powdered pigment. This is the time to do the painting if you so desire, and colors can be mixed to achieve the correct shade. Rub this in thoroughly, being careful not to get it on the areas which will remain natural color. In order to prevent the paint from rubbing off, a weak fixative should be mixed with the paint. When this is complete, you can proceed with the dress construction.

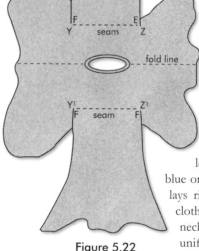

Figure 5.22

Although it was seldom done, if you want to have a contrasting-color cloth binding around the inside of the neck opening of your dress, add it before you continue with the sewing steps. Use a narrow (1" or less) strip of wool tradecloth in blue or red. Turn the yoke hide so it lays right side toward you. Fit the cloth around the edge of the oval neck opening. Taking very small uniform whip stitches; secure it. Work all the way around, back to where you began. Tie off the thread securely.

ATTACHING SKIRT TO YOKE

Look carefully at Figure 5.22, which illustrates how the skirt panels fit to the yoke of the three-skin dress. Points E and F of one skirt panel will coordinate with Points Y and Z on one side of the piece. Points E and F of the other skirt panel will coordinate with Points Y' and Z' on the other side. With the same texture

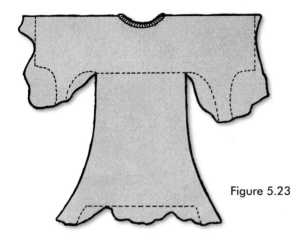

Figure 5.23

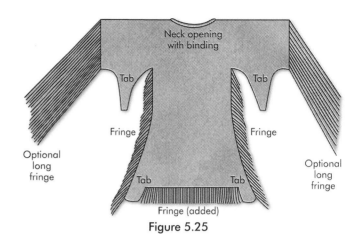

Figure 5.25

side of both hides facing each other, sew one skirt panel to one side of the yoke. Use a combination running and whip stitch with a ¼" seam allowance. Keep the stitches snug and small but be sure not to pull them too tightly, for the leather will roll. Repeat with the other skirt panel and yoke edge. Lay out dress as in Figure 5.22.

To complete the side seams of the garment, turn the leather so the wrong side is up and then pick up the dress by the shoulders. Position the skirt panels so they lay exactly on top of each other (with the right sides facing inside, toward each other). Insert two fringe strips between the edges of the skirt panels, with the ¼" uncut edges laying even with the edges of the panels. The fringe is sandwiched between the skirt panels as in Figure 5.6. Beginning at Point E, sew this side seam together carefully, progressing downward to within 3" of the bottom, to allow for bottom fringing. Take a few back stitches and tie off the thread securely.

Remember, when you sew these side seams you are actually going through four thicknesses of leather. You may need to use an awl to punch holes for sewing. Do the seam on the other side the same way, sandwiching two layers of fringe between. Now, turn the garment right side out. The shape should be roughly like the outline in Figure 5.23. To achieve the more tailored "squared off" look of classic Southern Cheyenne, Southern Arapaho and Kiowa style three-skin dresses, you can trim the yoke and hemlines like the dotted line shown in Figure 5.23. It is traditional to retain the "tabs" under the sleeves and at either side of the bottom of the skirt panels.

A row of fine fringe should be added carefully along the bottom edge of both skirt panels. This bottom fringe can be self-fringe or added in a number of ways. If desired, a row of long fringe can be sewn along the "wrist ends" of the sleeves, as illustrated in Figure 5.24. Pow wow dresses often have fringe along the sleeves that is over a yard in length. It is also common for these dresses to have at least one row of ornamental thongs (which are usually doubled) across the middle of the skirt panels, as shown in Figure 5.26. Decorate as befits tribal style.

Figure 5.24 Southern Cheyenne buckskin child's dress, ca. 1910, with typical, late period decoration. Courtesy of Maj. Gen. Michael C. Kostlenik, USAF (Ret.). Photo by Michael Kostelnik.

Figure 5.26 Detail of a common method of attaching decorative thongs across the skirt panel; from the the Comanche dress in Figure 6.3. Courtesy of Reddick Collection. Photo by Andy Russell

19th Century Plains Indian Dresses

SOUTHERN CHEYENNE & ARAPAHO
Accessories

The oldest type of Southern Cheyenne moccasin was the one piece side-seam. "A durable rawhide sole" was sometimes sewn to the outside for added protection (Hoebel, 1960:63). Abert notes this practice in his 1845 journal. *Shon-ka-mah-to*, a Cheyenne warrior, wished to give his beautifully beaded moccasins to Abert as a gift. Abert writes: "In this country they are obliged to sole (their moccasins) to protect the feet against numerous cacti. These soles are of 'parfleche' — the inside edge cut perfectly straight, and the toe pointed" (Abert 1846:10), which approximates the sole shape of side-seam moccasins. Knee-length leggings made from tanned deer, antelope, or elk hide accompanied the moccasins, and were held up with a leather garter (Grinnell, 1972:224). Early period leggings were often painted (yellow or green) and fringed at the bottom and up the sides. Sometimes they "had a side panel of quillwork" (Paterek, 1994:101).

As early as the 1840s, Cheyenne women were sometimes connecting their moccasins and leggings together. In speaking

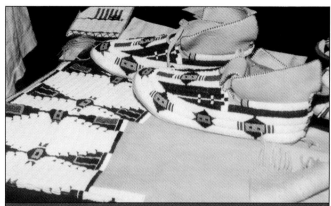

Figure 5.28 Classic pair of matching Southern Cheyenne moccasins and leggings, made by Maj. Gen. Michael C. Kostelnik, USAF (Ret). Photo by Michael Kostelnik.

of a Southern Cheyenne woman, Garrard noted "from the knee downward (her leg) was encased in a tightly fitting legging terminating in a neat moccasin — both handsomely worked with beads" (Garrard, 1955:54). Of his portrait subject *Mis-Stan-Star*, Abert wrote: "her beautiful leggings, which extended only to the knee, were so nicely joined with the moccasin that the connection could not be perceived, and looked as neat as the stockings of our eastern belles" (Abert, 1846:4). These Cheyenne "boots", or hightop moccasins, later were highly decorated with paint and beadwork, and metal buttons or conchos. Usually, the legging section of the moccasin is tall enough to reach above the knee if pulled completely up. Typically this extra area is fringed and worn turned down over the garter tie.

Cheyenne women were known for the beauty of their quilled wearing robes. Such quilled robes are within the realm of the sacred work produced by members of the Cheyenne quilling guilds. Therefore, it is essential to approach the re-creation of this type of item with utmost respect. A painted robe in typical Cheyenne patterns would be an acceptable alternative for the early 19th century look. Apparently, by at least the 1840s, Cheyenne women were acquiring and making use of Navaho blankets as outerwear. In 1845, Lt. Abert observed a large group of Cheyenne women dancing. They were all "cloaked with Navajo blankets" (Ibid:4). A trade blanket or wearing blanket and plaid, fringed shawls became common in the later 1800s.

Early 19th century Cheyenne belts were made of rawhide. By the mid 1800s, belts of harness leather decorated with brass tacks or bright metal "conchos" were becoming popular. These often had a long side "drop" similarly decorated. Women often wore leather tool cases tied to their belts. Of assorted shape and size, these cases/bags were used to keep various sewing and personal necessities handy (Hoebel, 1960:63).

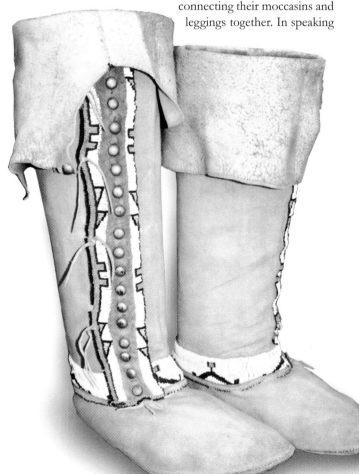

Figure 5.27 Southern Cheyenne or Arapaho hightop moccasins, ca. 1890. Courtesy of Reddick Collection.

According to first source journals and artwork, Cheyenne women were fond of jewelry, and were often quite lavish in their wearing of it. In his description of Cheyenne women who were taking part in a ceremonial dance, Garrard notes that "rings and bracelets of shining brass encircled their tapering arms and fingers, and shells dangled from their ears" (Garrard, 1955:85). In another journal entry, Garrard cites "bracelets of brass" on their arms, and "in their pierced ears" pendants made of shells from the Pacific shore" (Ibid:54). Carvalho saw Cheyenne women wearing bracelets of "brass wire or thin silver" (Carvalho, 1973:67). As with the Comanche, Cheyenne women typically wore necklaces and bracelets in multiples.

Cheyenne women often wore their hair parted in the middle with two long braids. They were also fond of painting their faces. This practice caused Garrard to write that the "fine complexions" of Cheyenne women were often "eclipsed by a coat of flaming vermilion" (Ibid:54).

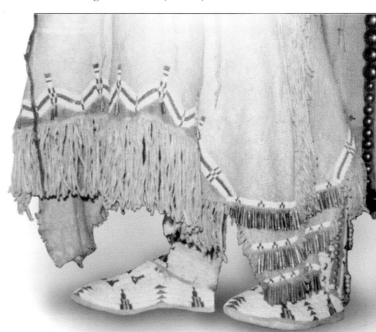

Figure 5.30 Detail of hem, moccasins and leggings. Courtesy Museum of the Plains Indian, Buffalo Bill Historical Society, Cody Wyoming. Photo by Susan Jennys.

Figure 5.29 Complete Cheyenne woman's outfit made in 1870's style by Michael Terry. (Note: knife sheath is not typical Cheyenne style) Photograph courtesy of Michael Terry.

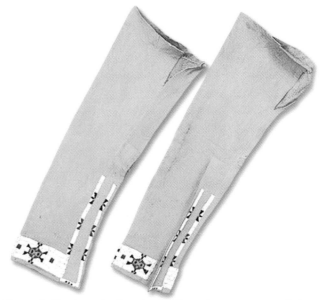

Figure 5.31. **Arapaho Leggings** – These leggings are made from brain-tanned buckskin that has been colored yellow with powder paint and beaded in size 5/0 Italian seed beads in white, black, greasy yellow and white-lined red. Courtesy of Reddick Collection.

19th Century Plains Indian Dresses

CHARACTERISTICS OF HISTORIC CHEYENNE, ARAPAHO & KIOWA DRESSES

A Brief Comparison

The mid-to-late 19th Century dresses of certain Southern Plains tribes can often appear alike, especially to the beginning craftsman. The following information is presented in an effort to help the reader become more aware of the often subtle differences between Cheyenne and Kiowa styles. As you read, please keep in mind that this study is deliberately brief and not all-inclusive. The reader is encouraged to use this section as a springboard to undertake his or her own more extensive comparative study.

As similar as they might appear, there were often minor variations in the "cut" of these dresses which were somewhat characteristic of the given tribal group. For instance, while both Cheyenne and Kiowa dresses had large, squared yokes with the leg hide left pendant-like on the underside of the sleeves, the bottom edge of the yoke of Kiowa garments was often cut in scallops. Rather than the Cheyenne-style straight-cut bottom edge with a scalloped pattern above it in paint and beads, the Kiowa dress often had the hem itself scalloped, with a row of fringe added beneath it (Paterek, 1994:118). Although understanding such variations in dress cut is certainly helpful in interpreting tribal style, it is largely their decoration that sets the historic dresses of one tribe apart from another.

Whereas a Cheyenne dress might be painted yellow on the yoke with smaller painted areas (in a contrasting darker hue) at neck and hem, Kiowa dresses were sometimes "painted all over, either yellow or a combination of yellow and green" (Op Cite:116). Furthermore, both tribes might put beadwork on their dresses, but there was a distinct difference in the layout and the extent to which it was used. The Southern Cheyenne decorated their dresses with "scalloped lines of beading at the lower edge" (Conn, 1982:142) and "wide bands of bead embroidery" across the yoke and shoulders, in "more solid and massive figures" (Conn, 1976:84).

Both Kiowa and Comanche women seemed to prefer to paint their dresses and or to ornament them with scalloping, than to decorate them with large areas of beadwork. They applied beadwork quite sparingly. In fact, unlike their Sioux or Crow counterparts to the north, the Kiowa and Comanche rarely produced any item that was heavily beaded — the notable exception being cradles (Conn, 1976:83; Hail, 2000:26-29). On Kiowa dresses, beadwork was limited to narrow trim and edgings, and an occasional tiny rosette. According to Richard Conn, the Comanche were often even more reserved in their use of beadwork than the Kiowa (Ibid:84).

In trying to understand the differences between tribal styles, it is important to remember that no single factor, by itself, should be considered to determine the style of a given dress. For instance, Cheyenne, Arapaho and Kiowa women sometimes ornamented a dress with multiple horizontal rows of money cowrie shells or elk teeth. Both tribes considered these

Figure 5.32 This fine Comanche or Kiowa dress is made of brain-tanned buckskin and features cowrie shells on the yoke, with tin cone, paint, ribbon, horse hair and beadwork decoration. Courtesy Morning Star Gallery. Photo by Rex Reddick.

shells and teeth expensive and difficult to come by. Dress yokes covered with them had high monetary value and brought the owner a measure of social distinction (Ewers, 1979:78). But because women of both tribes used these ornaments, this decorative characteristic alone will not suffice to determine a garment's tribal style. A garment has a correct Cheyenne-Arapaho (or Kiowa, or Comanche) "look" because it exhibits a number of appropriate tribal characteristics, it is accompanied by accessories also characteristic of that tribe. Historically there were a limited number of dressmakers (at least among the Kiowa), which must surely have contributed to a common tribal style.

Figure 5.33 Southern Cheyenne or Arapaho style dress made by Mike Kostelnik. Complete with German silver concho belt and drag (or drop), beaded belt set and fully beaded moccasins. Note the placement of the bags on the belt, which is normally specific to each tribe. Courtesy of Maj. Gen. Michael C. Kostelnik, USAF (Ret). Photo by Michael Kostelnik.

Figure 5.34
Cheyenne dress made from blue saved list cloth with the selvage retained as ornamentation. The dress is accented with ribbons, brass sequins, and rows of money cowrie shells. Note the gussets seen hanging below the hemline on either side of the garment, and the short rows of shells oriented vertically in the shoulder areas. A tack belt is a perfect accouterment for the tradecloth dress. Belt and dress both date from the early 20th century. Courtesy of the Benson Lanford Collection. Photo by Benson Lanford.

Chapter 6:

DAUGHTERS' DRESSES & AFTERTHOUGHTS

The dominant consideration of this book has been *women's* clothing; historically-styled garments and accessories to fit the adult female. But what about the young ladies of re-enacting and the powwow circuits? What types of garments are they to wear? Let's spend a moment looking at the special needs of young women ... our daughters and granddaughters. We will begin with the youngest and work our way up in age.

What were infants wearing in the the Plains Indian villages of the early 1800's? Most primary evidence would answer, "Very little - if anything". The early source journals of Euro-American traders and explorers who initially encountered Plains peoples, are replete with references to the *au naturale* mode of dress for most young children. As with our modern practice, infants in the historic Plains village were lovingly wrapped in special blankets and robes. A robe not only kept the child warm, but - through an elaborately and lovingly painted symbolism, reminded the child (and the adults around her) of the love of her family and her special place within the universe. A robe was also versatile. It could be used as a blanket or as an impromptu over-mom's-hip or over-big-sister's-back baby carrier. Hence, a soft elk or deerskin robe, perhaps painted in a box and border, or border-and-hourglass design, is the fundamental article of "clothing" for the infant. It should also be noted here that there was a great deal of difference in the clothing of the children in a family. An almost universal trait was that the "favorite child", or sometimes the first born son, received the finest.

Figure 6.1 Southern Plains Indian Girl with melons, by German frontier artist F. R. Petri, circa 1835. Although a valuable example of an early dress, this appears exceptionally short for the modest styles among Southern Plains women of this period. Courtesy Texas Memorial Museum. Photo 2281-1.

DAUGHTERS' DRESSES

The second-most important historic "garment" for the infant is a traditional cradle or cradleboard. Historically, cradles were highly functional yet perfectly adornable gifts with which to honor the new-born and its parents. Speaking as a mom *and* active living history participant, I encourage mothers and grandmothers to make use of the cradle whenever and wherever it is appropriate. As infants, my children spent much of their time at living history events happily looking out at the world from the safety and security of a cradleboard. For me, making and learning the efficient use of the cradleboard proved to be a wonderful "connection" point which bridged my new role as a mother with my passion for re-enactment. My children enjoyed their outings through camp. Did you know that the cure for a fussy infant isn't a ride in the car ... it's a ride in the cradle-board! Many other folks in the camp, re-enactors and public alike, thoroughly enjoyed their outings, too. In my humble opinion, there's absolutely nothing as beautiful at a powwow or living history event, as a well-dressed mother with her infant daughter in a quilled or beaded cradleboard.

Figure 6.2 Katie Roubideaux, age 8. Katie's mother was a Rosebud Sioux and her father was the interpreter Louis Roubideaux. She was photographed by John A. Anderson in 1898, wearing her beautifully beaded buckskin dress, fully beaded leggings and moccasins. Courtesy Nebraska Historical Society, Photo No. RG 2969.

While she is snugged securely inside a cradle, a child has little need for clothing *per se*. But what about the rest of the time? On those occasions where a tiny garment is warranted, a simple cape, made from a small deerskin (chamois works well, too) with a head-hole cut from the center, should suffice nicely. Infants and toddlers are by nature active, and they possess an amazingly strong dirt magnet. They also outgrow their clothing very rapidly. Budget-conscious parents would do well to follow the principal: *the simpler, the better*. Save the fancily decorated buckskin outfits for the older child.

Speaking of decorations and protective charms, please be aware that any adornment device like small beads and long narrow fringe can be lovely on historic garments, but for the tiny child it can also be lethal. Small beads, shells, animal teeth, fluffy feathers and long narrow fringes, etc. are all potentially dangerous because they are choking hazards. Consequently, these items should **not** be part of the tiny tots' outfit. In fact, to play it safe, such decorative devices should probably be avoided altogether until the child and her playmates are safely past the put-everything-in-the-mouth stage. Should you wish to honor a new-born in your family with a special gift of a specially adorned outfit, it would be best to offer the family a *token* such as a doll-sized miniature of the garment that will later be presented to the *toddler*.

So far we've addressed the garmenting of the tiny tot. But what about the young ladies from post-toddlerhood through the teen years? What type of historic garments are most appropriate for them to wear to a re-enactment or powwow? Historic precedent from most Great Plains tribes clearly points to one fact: young ladies basically wore the same things the older women did - except that they were "scaled down" for their smaller size. In short: young ladies should resemble the older ones. I like to refer to this principle as: **Mom - in miniature.**

When individually hand crafting garments, items are typically fitted and modeled or "tailor-made" to the intended wearer. Taking careful measurements is the most important step to insure a perfect-fitting finished product. This holds true for creating children's wear as well as adults'. Then it's a matter of scaling down the measurements in a systematic manner. Creating scaled-down garments based on full-size adult examples is relatively easy. Using an adult size pattern for comparison, the seamstress needs to determine the correct proportion ratio relative to the child in comparison. In other words, if mom's dress measures 50 inches from shoulder to hemline, and daughter is one-half mom's height, daughter's dress will measure around 25 inches from shoulder to hemline. If daughter is two-third mom's height, her dress will measure about 33 inches.

The well-dressed young lady representative of the early 1800's might sport; a side seam dress, leggings and moccasins, a painted robe, a belt and "belt set" (for the smallest children, edged tools should be diminutive only!), and appropriate jewelry or personal adornment items (necklaces, rings, bracelets). As with her adult counterparts, she should also have an assortment of carefully made historically viable "play-things" like dolls, miniature tipi and parfleches, etc., and her own camp accessories such as a "possible" or tipi bag, sewing kit, etc.

One of the most charming things I have ever encountered at a re-enactment was a grandmother-mother-daughter-daughter's doll quartet, wearing matching buckskin dresses, leggings, and moccasins. Even my daughter and I, when sporting matching tradewool dresses with elktooth decoration, have turned a few heads with appreciative smiles. Outfit your daughter as you would outfit yourself - with the same attention to historic detail, quality stitching, and aesthetically pleasing decoration. She need not be a "carbon copy" of you - and in fact, I do not encourage exact duplication. But she could be wearing the same types of things as mom, **and** she should be shown how to wear them with dignity and honor.

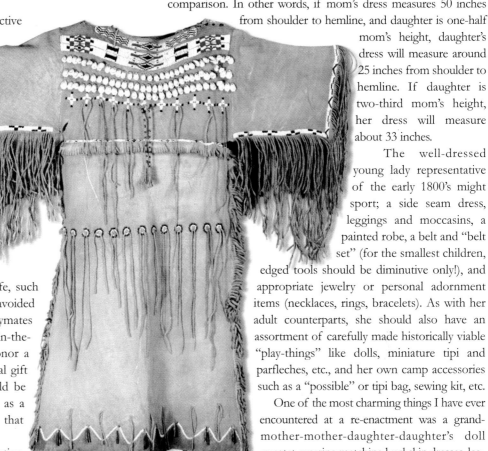

Figure 6.3 Comanche Girl's Dress
This exquisite dress was made for the daughter of Quanah Parker when she was approximately 6 years old. Made of soft, native tanned buckskin that is lightly smoked, it is decorated with red, white and blue seed beads, buckskin fringe, money cowrie shells, tin cones, green paint and a small mink or ermine skin with feet and legs intact. Courtesy of the Reddick Collection. Photo by Andy Russell.

19th Century Plains Indian Dresses

19ᵗʰ Century Plains Indian Dresses
AFTERTHOUGHTS

As fascinating as it may be to try to trace the development and dissemination of Plains Indian dress styles throughout the 19th century, it is important to emphasize the fact that up until the mid-1800s distinct tribal styles are often difficult to identify with certainty. Many pre-1850 artifacts simply defy exact identification; every "authority" who examines them offers a different conclusion about date and tribe of origin. Rather than trying to pin them with a specific tribal attribution, such artifacts might be better understood in a regional perspective. Many of these artifacts do fit within the succession of regional traits popular during certain time periods. However, it must also be stressed that even the regional traits identified by ethnologists are far from universal in scope. What's more, just like tribal traits, regional ones also tend to overlap and evolve. This is a "fluidity" of fashion caused primarily by two factors: material trade (commodities) and people trade (intermarriage, adoption of captives, slavery, etc.).

Intertribal trade routes existed long before the coming of the Europeans. Various centers of material trade existed throughout the Great Plains, including those among the village peoples of the Upper Missouri, and the Shoshoni people of the central Rockies. Regionally, these tribes were situated in an advantageous (and consequently oftentimes dangerous) position as middlemen -- those through whom there was a multi-directional flow of goods, and therefore cultural ideas and expressions. Clothing styles were affected by this flow and interchange. Some tribes were particularly noted for their fine tanning, excellent sewing skills, and beautiful garments. Tanned hides and finished clothing became objects of admiration and trade between tribes. Hence, "fashion" changed hands two hundred years ago like it does today. What we think of as "Shoshoni" may have been "Crow" twenty years earlier, or "Mandan" twenty years before that (Bell, 1957:239).

On the Great Plains, people trade undoubtedly contributed to the exchange and adoption of material culture and social ideas. Members of some tribes intermarried. Most tribes took captives, especially women and children, who were regularly assimilated and sometimes formally adopted into their captors' societies. The ideas and creative forms most familiar to these people went with them into their new world. In short, it was impossible for material culture to remain static.

So how does this apply to re-creating the Plains Indian garments featured in this book? Hopefully, the crafters goal is to produce a historically viable garment that can be correctly identified by others. For instance, when you make a Crow style outfit and wear it to an

Figure 6.4 The wife of Spotted Tail, a Brule Lakota, by Alexander Gardner, Washington, DC, 1872. This photo clearly shows that by this time the Sioux were producing dresses with fully beaded yokes, although designs were less elaborate than found in later periods. Note the striped blanket she is wearing. Smithsonian Photo, Negative #NAA-3120A.

event, you hope to hear comments affirming a correct Crow "look". Approaching this task with integrity takes a lot of research and careful planning, so do your best to saturate yourself with historical information. Read the literature, visit many museums, talk to respected elders and accomplished craftsmen, etc.. But the re-creation task is more than memorizing data and translating it into your craftwork. The task also requires humility and an open mind. When it comes to times past, sometimes the best we can do is to make an educated guess.

Have fun with your research. Take the time to enjoy the creative process. Learn from your mistakes. And above all, share your experiences with others.

Bibliography

Abert, Lt. James W. *Bents Fort to St. Louis in 1845*. Washington, D.C: SENATE EXECUTIVE DOCUMENT #49;1846, 32nd Congress, 1st Session, (1846) 275.

—. *Through The Country of The Comanche Indians In The Fall of the Year 1845: Journal of a U.S. Army Expedition Led by Lt. John W. Abert*. Ed., John Galvin. San Francisco: John Howell Books, 1970.

American Fur Company. American Fur Company Papers, 1829-1851. St. Louis, MO: Missouri Historical Society, n.d.

Batkin, Jonathan. *Splendid Heritage*. Santa Fe, NM: Wheelright Museum of the American Indian, 1995.

Bell, John R. *The Journal of Captain John R. Bell, The Far West and the Rocky Mountains 1820-1875, Vol. 6.* Ed., Harlin M. Fuller and LeRoy R. Hafen. Glendale, CA: Arthur H. Clark Company, 1957.

Bemiss, Elijah. *The Dyer's Companion*. New York, NY: Evert Duhckinck, 1815.

Berlandier, Jean Louis. *The Indians of Texas in 1830*. Ed., John C. Ewers. Washington, D.C: Smithsonian Institution Press, 1969.

Biddle, Nicholas, Editor. *The Journals of Lewis & Clark*. (Two Volumes) New York, NY: Heritage Press, 1962.

Brafford, C. J., & Laine Thom. *Dancing Colors: Paths of Native American Women*. San Francisco, CA: Chronicle Books, 1992.

Brown, David L. *Three Years in the Rocky Mountains* NEWS OF THE PLAINS AND THE ROCKIES; Vol 1. Ed., David A. White. Spokane, WA: Arthur H. Clark Company, 1996.

Cahoon, Sam. 2002. Personal correspondence.

Carroll, H. Bailey & J. Villasana Haggard. *Three New Mexico Chronicles*. Albuquerque, NM: Quivira Society, 1942.

Carvalho, Solomon N. *Incidents of Travel and Adventure in the Far West*. New York, NY: Arno Press, 1973.

Catlin, George. *Letters and Notes on the Manners, Customs, and Conditions of North American Indians*. (Two Volumes) New York, NY: Dover Publications, Inc., 1973.

Conn, Richard. *A Classification of Aboriginal North American Clothing*. Unpublished Master's Thesis. Seattle, WA: Univ. of Washington Press, 1955

—. *Blackfeet Women's Clothing* WHISPERING WIND CRAFTS ANNUAL #2, New Orleans, LA: Written Heritage, 1989.

—. *Circles of the World*. Denver, CO: Denver Art Museum, 1982.

—. *Southern Plains Beadwork in the Fred Harvey Fine Arts Collection* The Fred Harvey Fine Arts Collection. Phoenix, AZ: Heard Museum. 1976.

Cox, Ross. *Adventures on the Columbia River*. New York, NY: J & J Harper Company, 1832.

Dale, Harrison Clifford. *The Ashley-Smith Explorations and the Discovery of a Central Route to the Pacific, 1822-1829, with the Original Journals*. Cleveland, OH: The Arthur H. Clark Company, 1918.

Denig, Edwin Thompson, *Five Indian Tribes of the Upper Missouri: Sioux, Arickaras, Assiniboines, Crees, Crows*. Norman, OK: University of Oklahoma Press, 1961

DeSmet, Father Pierre Jean. *Letters and Sketches: With a Narrative of a Year's Residence Among the Indian Tribes of the Rocky Mountains* EARLY WESTERN TRAVELS. Vol 27. Cleveland, OH: Arthur H. Clark Co., 1906.

DeVoto, Bernard, Editor. *The Journals of Lewis & Clark*. Boston, MA: Houghton Mifflin Company, 1953.

Ewers, John C. *Climate, Acculturation, and Costume: A History of Women's Clothing Among the Indians of the Southern Plains* PLAINS ANTHROPOLOGIST, n.s. 25(87) (1979), pp 63-82.

—. *Blackfeet Crafts* INDIAN HANDCRAFTS 9. Washington, D.C: Bureau of Indian Affairs, Dept. of the Interior, 1945.

—. *Plains Indian History and Culture: Essays on Continuity and Change*. Norman, OK: University of Oklahoma Press, 1997.

Farnham, Thomas J. *Travels in the Great Western Prairies*. (Two Volumes). New York, NY: DaCapo Reprints, 1973.

Fecteau, Susan. *Primitive Indian Dresses*. Springfield, OR: Green River Forge, Ltd. 1979.

Feder, Norman. *The Side Fold Dress* AMERICAN INDIAN ART MAGAZINE, (Winter 1984), 48-55, 75-77.

Ferris, Warren Angus. *Life in the Rocky Mountains*. Ed., Paul C. Phillips. Denver, CO: Old West Publishing Company, 1940.

First Voices, NEBRASKALAND MAGAZINE 62(1) (Jan.-Feb. 1984), Lincoln, NE: Nebraska Games & Parks Commission, 1984.

Garrard, Lewis H. *WahToYah and the Taos Trail*. Norman, OK: University of Oklahoma Press, 1955.

Gass, Patrick. *A Journal of the Voyages and Travels of Captains Lewis and Clark, 1804-1806*. Minneapolis, MN: Ross & Haines Inc. 1958.

Grinnell, George Bird. *The Cheyenne Indians: Their History and Ways of Life*. Lincoln, NE: Univ. of Nebraska Press, 1923.

Hail, Barbara A., *Gifts of Pride and Love: Kiowa and Comanche Cradles*. Bristol, RI: Haffenreffer Museum of Anthropology, Brown University, 2000.

Hanson, Charles E., Jr. *Pound Beads, Pony Beads* THE MUSEUM OF THE FUR TRADE QUARTERLY 25(4) (Winter 1989), 17.

—. *Printed Calicos for Indians* THE MUSEUM OF THE FUR TRADE QUARTERLY 24(3) (Fall 1988), 8.

Hanson, James A., & Kathryn Wilson. *Feminine Fur Trade Fashion*. Chadron, NE: The Fur Press, 1976.

Harmon, Daniel W. *Journal of Voyages & Travels in the Interior of North America*. New York, NY: A. S. Barnes, 1903.

Hoebel, E. Adamson. *The Cheyennes: Indians of the Great Plains*. New York, NY: Holt, Rinehart & Winston, Inc., 1960.

Holm, Bill. *Plains Indian Cloth Dresses* AMERICAN INDIAN HOBBYIST 4(5 & 6) (Jan-Feb 1958), 43-47.

How to Make Moccasins: Volume 1: Plains Indian Hard Sole Style. Dir. Swearingen, Scott and Sandy Rhoades. Full Circle Communications, 1997.

Hungry Wolf, Adolf & Beverly Hungry Wolf. *Blackfoot Craftworker's Book* (2nd Edition).Skookumchuck, British Columbia, Canada: Good Medicine Books, 1977.

Jennys, Susan. *Getting Down To Brass Tacks* MUZZLE BLASTS 56(7) (March 1995), 11-14.

—. *Practical Advice For Making a Plains Styled Buckskin Dress* MUZZLE BLASTS 54(8) (April 1993), 40-45.

—. *Robes: Wrapping Yourself in the Past* MUZZLELOADER 20(2) (May,June 1993), 33-35.

Johnson, Cathy. *Walk Softly: Moccasins in the Context of the Primary Documents.* St. Louis, MO: Graphics/Fine Arts Press, 1996

Koch, Ronald P. *Dress Clothing of the Plains Indians.* Norman, OK: University of Oklahoma Press, 1977.

Kurz, Rudolph Frederick. *The Journal of Rudolph F. Kurz 1846-1852.* Ed., J. N. B. Hewitt. BULLETIN #115, Smithsonian Institute, Bureau of American Ethnology. Washington D.C: U.S. Government Printing Office (1937), 13-48 (+ Plates).

Lanford, Benson. *Historic Plains Indian Jewelry,* AMERICAN INDIAN ART MAGAZINE 18(4) (Autumn 1993), 64-72, 99.

Larocque, Francois. *The Journal of Fransois Larocque From the Assiniboine to the Yellowstone in 1805.* Ed., L. J. Burpee. CANADIAN ARCHIVES PUBLICATIONS #3. Ottawa: Canadian Archives, 1910.

Lessard, Rosemary T. *A Short Historical Survey of Lakota Women's Clothing* PLAINS INDIAN DESIGN SYMBOLOGY & DECORATION. Ed., Gene Ball & George P. Horse Capture. Cody, WY: Buffalo Bill Historical Center, 1980.

Little, Shan. *A Sioux Woman's Dentalium Shell Dress* AMERICAN INDIAN CRAFTS & CULTURE 2(10) (1968), 46.

Lowie, Robert H. *Crow Indian Art* ANTHROPOLOGICAL PAPERS (Vol. 21, Pt. 4). New York: American Museum of Natural History (1920).

—. *Crow Material Culture* ANTHROPOLOGICAL PAPERS (Vol. 23, Pt. 3). New York, NY: American Museum of Natural History (1922).

Mann, Julia de L. *The Cloth Industry in the West of England from 1640 to 1880,* Clarendon Press, Oxford, England: 1971.

Markoe, Glenn E., Editor. *Vestiges of a Proud Nation: The Ogden B. Read Northern Plains Indian Collection.* Burlington, VT: Robert Hull Fleming Museum, 1986

Mason, J. Alden. *A Collection From the Crow Indians* MUSEUM JOURNAL (Vol. 17), Univ. of Penn. (1926), 393-417.

Maximilian, Prince. *Travels in the Interior of North America 1832 1834* EARLY WESTERN TRAVELS XXII-XXIV. Ed., Reuben G. Thwaites. Cleveland, OH: Arthur H. Clark Company, 1906.

Merritt, Ann S. *Women's Beaded Robes: Artistic Reflections of the Crow World.* To Honor The Crow People. Ed., Father Peter J. Powell; Foundation for the Preservation of Indian Art and Culture. Chicago, IL, 1988, pp 40-47.

Partridge, William. *A Practical Treatise on Dying of Woollen, Cotton, and Skein Silk with the Manifacture of Broadcloth and Cassimere. New York,* NY: H. Wallis & Co, 1823.

Paterek, Josephine. *Encyclopedia of American Indian Costume.* New York, NY: W. W. Norton & Company, 1994

Peake, Ora Brooks. *A History of the United States Factory System 1795-1822.* Denver, CO: Sage Books, 1954.

Petri, F. R. *German Artist on the Texas Frontier.* Austin, TX: University of Texas Press, 1978.

Powers, Marla K. *Oglala Women.* Chicago, IL: University of Chicago Press, 1986.

Russell, Osborne. *Journal of a Trapper.* Ed., Aubrey L. Haines. Lincoln, NE: University of Nebraska Press, 1986.

Sage, Rufus. *Rocky Mountain Life.* Lincoln, NE: University of Nebraska Press, 1982.

Schneider, Mary Jane. *Plains Indian Clothing: Stylistic Persistence and Change* OKLAHOMA ANTHROPOLOGICAL SOCIETY BULLETIN Volume 17 (Nov 1968), p 155.

Shawley, Stephen D. *Nez Perce Dress: A Study in Culture Change.* Moscow, ID: University of Idaho, 1974

Smith, Cathy. *Fur Trade Indian Dresses,* BOOK OF BUCKSKINNING V Ed., William Scurlock. Texarkana, TX: Rebel Publishing Company (1989), 136.

Stearns, Robert E. C. *A Study of Primitive Money,* SMITHSONIAN INSTITUTION ANNUAL REPORT (1887). Washington, D.C., pp 315-320.

Tabeau, Pierre Antoine. *Tabeau's Narrative of Loisel's Expedition to the Upper Missouri.* Ed., Annie H. Abel. Norman, OK: University of Oklahoma Press, 1939.

Talbot, Theodore. *The Journals of Theodore Talbot: 1843 & 1849-1852.* Ed., Charles H. Carey. Portland, OR: MetroPress, 1931.

Taylor, Colin F. *Yupika: The Plains Indian Woman's Dress; An Overview of Historical Developmets and Styles.* Wyk auf Foehr, Germany: Verlag für Americkanistik, 1977.

Thomas, Davis & Karin Ronnefeldt. *People of the First Man.* New York, NY: E. P. Dutton & Company, 1976.

Thompson, David. *David Thompson's Narrative of His Explorations in Western America, 1784-1812.* Ed. by J. B. Tyrrell. Champlain Society Publication No. 12. Toronto 1916.

Tixier, Victor. *Tixier's Travels on the Osage Prairies 1839-1840.* Ed., John Francis McDermott. Norman, OK: University of Oklahoma Press, 1940.

Townsend, John K. *The Narrative of John K. Townsend* EARLY WESTERN TRAVELS (Vol. 19). Ed., Reuben G. Thwaites. Cleveland, OH: Arthur H. Clark Company, 1905.

Trudeau, JeanBaptiste. *The Narrative Journal of Jean Baptiste Trudeau* SOUTH DAKOTA HISTORICAL COLLECTIONS 7, (1914). Pierre, SD: South Dakota State Department of History, pp 40, 34, 67.

Weitzner, Bella. *Notes on the Hidatsa Indians Based on the Data Recorded by the Late Gilbert L. Wilson* ANTHROPOLOGICAL PAPERS Vol. 56, Part 2. New York: American Museum of Natural History (1979).

White, George M. *Craft Manual of North American Indian Footwear.* Arlee, MT: White Publishing, 1969.

Wissler, Clark. *Costumes of the Plains Indians* ANTHROPOLOGICAL PAPERS Vol. 17, Part 2. New York: American Museum of Natural History (1915), pp 47, 91.

—. *Material Culture of the Blackfoot Indians* ANTHROPOLOGICAL PAPERS Vol. 5, Part 1. New York, NY: American Museum of Natural History (1910).

—. *Structural Basis to the Decoration of Costumes Among the Plains Indians* ANTHROPOLOGICAL PAPERS Vol. 17, Part 3. New York: American Museum of Natural History (1916).